RAFEEQ REHMAN

I0008343

Cybersecurity Arm Wrestling

Winning the perpetual fight against crime by building a modern
Security Operations Center (SOC)

Copyright © 2019-21 Rafeeq U. Rehman

Limits on reproduction and distribution

This book is property of the author. No parts of this book can be modified, published or reproduced in any shape or form without written permission of the author and publisher. A pdf version of the book may be available at author's personal blog site rafeeqrehman.com. This is made available for personal use only and you are not allowed to publish it on any social media sites.

Trademarks and Servicemarks

Any trademark and service mark referenced in this book belong to their respective owners. Some images in this book are published under Creative Common License[7]. References to these images and other material are provided either in footnotes or in the Bibliography at the end of the book.

Contents

II   Building SOC   51

5   SOC Technology Stack   53

6   SOC Implementation Planning   69

List of Figures

List of Tables

Acknowledgments

This book could not be possible without generous help from many in the information security community throughout the process.

Following is list of people who provided reviews, comments and suggestions to make this book better (in alphabetical order).

- Aaron Woody has experience in SOC, building vulnerability management programs, threat intelligence, automation and many other areas. I am thankful for his insights, interviews, and recommendations.

- Andres Ricardo Almanza Junco provided many useful suggestions for improvement in the manuscript. Thank you Andres!

- Atif Yusuf, with his vast CISO experience and industry knowledge, not only provided useful insights but also connected me with others in the industry for further research.

- Chad Sturgill graciously accpted my invite for phone interviews and provided many gems from his experience.

- Dan Bunner is a highly experience security professionals and I have been benefiting from his expertise for more than fifteen years. Thank you Dan for providing reviews!

- Eric Tremblay reviewed many chapters and provided his input to make improvements.

- Eric Zielinski has experience in running SOC at a major financial services organization. He provided his input into what are necessary skils for SOC analyst.

- Jeff Harrison provided very valuable input from his experience of build successful SOC. Thank you Jeff!

- Kim Behn managed SOC at multiple organizations. Her insights into operational pitfalls and managing SOC shifts were very interesting and useful.

- Mick Leach provided valuable insights into his experience of designing, planning and operating SOC

- Phillip Crump reviewed almost all of the book very thoroughly. Without his input, it would be impossible to finalize this manuscript. I am really thankful to Phillip Crump for his insights into many topics, thorough reviews, and correcting many language mistakes to make the manuscript better readable. If you see correct use of "article", it is because of Phillip as this is one of my major weakness when it comes to English grammar. Thank you Phillip!

- Yasir Khalid brought his knowledge and experience in collecting threat intelligence and put it into practice as well as provided his point of view on what a futuristic security operations center should look like.

There are many who helped in one way or the other to make this book happen. I have received advice from many of you through LinkedIn and Twitter on different aspects of security operations. Although it is difficult to mention everyone here but I just wanted to acknowledge them. Keep it up!

Last but not the least, I have read hundreds of research papers, reports, articles, and blog posts from broader information security community. I am thankful to all of these people who work hard to share their findings for the benefit of the community.

Thanks to LaTeX Community

If you find typesetting of this book pleasing to your eyes, it is not by accident. This is because of the LaTeX[1] typesetting system and a large community of LaTeXusers around the world. LaTeX, which is based upon TeX, developed by Donald Knuth, enables creating large documents like this one, as well as creating indexing and cross references. I am extremely thankful to this community to continuously build and evolve this open source typesetting system that brings joy to not only reading beautiful document but also to create them.

---

[1]https://www.latex-project.org/

Preface

This book has been a work-in-progress for quite some time and it looks like it will remain the same. Reason? Cybersecurity is a continuously evolving field and despite continuous efforts by the industry, I have not heard of anybody inventing a silver bullet to address emerging threats. Not even close! So the work continues...

Security Operations Center or SOC plays a key role in combating Cybersecurity threats. Many public and private sector organizations have built Security Operations Centers in-house whereas others have outsourced SOC operations to managed security services providers. Some also choose a hybrid approach by keeping parts of SOC operations in-house and outsourcing the rest of it. However, many of these efforts don't bring the intended results or realize desired business outcomes.

This book is an effort to learn from experiences of many SOC practitioners and researchers to find practices that have been proven to be useful while avoiding common pitfalls in building SOC. I have also explored different ideas to find a "balanced" approach towards building a SOC and making informed choices between functions that can/should be kept in-house and the ones that can be outsourced.

Cybersecurity is a Perpetual Arm Wrestling

Practitioners in Cybersecurity community understand that they are an unending war with opponents who have varying interests, but are mostly motivated by financial gains [42]. New vulnerabilities are continuously discovered, new technologies are continuously being developed, and attackers are innovative in exploiting flaws to gain access to information assets for financial gains. It is profitable for attackers to succeed only few times. In essence, you as a security professional, are continuously trying to defeat your opponents while they are relentless in their efforts. Hopefully you win this *perpetual arm wrestling* most of the times, but keep in mind that sometimes you will lose as well on preparedness for detection, incident response, and recovery for those situations while continuously working on identification and protection at the same time. You are in a *perpetual arm wrestling*!

Book Audience

Security Operations Center (SOC) plays a key role in this perpetual arm wrestling to ensure you win most of the times. And if you fail once in a while, you can get back very quickly without much damage. People, who are part of SOC planning, architecture, design, implementation, operations, and incidents response will find this book useful. Even if you are an experienced SOC professional, you will still find few interesting ideas as I have done significant research and interviewed many SOC professionals to include tips to help avoid pitfalls. This book is also a window into my experience of last fifteen years in helping businesses of all sizes build security operations centers.

- **CISOs** will benefit from chapters related to planning, business case development and budgeting information.

- **SOC Architects** - People who are responsible for designing and building security operations center will learn about how to design SOC, pros and cons of different SOC models, and how to avoid pitfalls.

- **SOC Managers** - The security operations center managers will be able to benefit from information related to SOC job roles, 24x7x365 staff scheduling, training, building knowledgebase, and many other areas related to SOC operations.

- **Corporate and Cybersecurity Leaders** - You may get a better idea about budgeting, metrics, dashboards and reporting.

I am sure that insights presented in this book will be beneficial for *all* information security professionals even if your regular work is not related to SOC.

Purpose of Book

This books is written with following key objectives in mind:

- Understand what it takes to build a SOC, both from financial and people perspective

- Decide which SOC model works better for you (insourced, outsourced, or a hybrid)

- Make your SOC project successful and avoid pitfalls

- Learn from experience of others

- Help you improve any existing SOC

- Cover emerging technologies and threat intelligence

- Continuous SOC improvement

Book Organization

The books ir organized in three parts, with multiple chapters in each part. The book start with introduction and development of business case and then move to building and operations of SOC. The last part of the book is about continuous improvement of SOC over a period of time. Following is a brief summary of three parts.

- **Part I - SOC Planning**, covers introduction to SOC, building business case and budget

- **Part II - Building SOC**, covers everything from architecture, design, building and operations

- **Part III - Continuous Improvement**, is about continuous improvement including threat hunting and developing meaningful metrics

What this Book is not about

The field of information security is evolving and responsibilities of information security leaders are expanding over time as I have been describing in CISO MindMap[2]. This book is not to cover all aspects of information security program and has a very narrow focus on SOC. For

---

[2]See CISO MindMap at my blog http://rafeeqrehman.com

example, this is not about how you will configure firewalls or IPS or proxy servers. Neither it is about establishing a vulnerability management program or patching systems. However, we do use log data coming from security devices, system logs, and information from vulnerability scans in SOC operations (among other types of data). Basically we are focused on how to glean intelligence from a multitude of data sources, correlations, identifying interesting events and managing incident lifecycle. Everything else is out of scope of this book.

Security operations centers employ many tools. Hands-on configuration information of these tools and technologies is covered well in accompanying manuals as well as other sources available on the Internet. For example, in my view there is no point in discussing how to configure a Syslog client. You will not find this type of information in the book. Avoiding these hand-on details discussion is helping keep this book shorter.

What is Next?

There are some future sections/chapters for this book which will be added in the next edition/revision. Most important of the planned improvements include:

- Adding more diagrams
- SOC metrics

Stay tuned for future enhancements. I have not yet decided about how frequently I will make these enhancement but I can say that these will be at least once a year.

Getting Latest Copy of Book

This book is available in both electronic and print formats (draft versions only in PDF format). The plan is to update the book on yearly basis to ensure all latest developments are covered. Always check for the latest version of this book on my personal blog site rafeeqrehman.com.

Your Feedback and Comments

Your feedback is important to me. Send your comments on my blog site rafeeqrehman.com or direct message on Twitter handle @rafeeq_rehman.

Part I

SOC Planning

— A journey of a thousand miles begins with a single step.

A Chinese proverb

— Without a measureless and perpetual uncertainty, the drama of human life would be destroyed.

Winston Churchill

1

Introduction

Protecting confidentiality and integrity of data, while ensuring availability of digital assets and key technology systems is crucial for operating any business in the bold new hyper-connected universe. An effective Security Operations Center (SOC) is a primary means and plays a key role to achieve this goal. As the newer technologies like machine learning, IoT, Blockchain, autonomous and connected vehicles and others are becoming crucial for business success, the concept of a modern SOC is also going through an evolution process. A modern SOC must provide capability to effectively manage risk associated with traditional as well as emerging technologies.

This book is a brief guideline for information security leaders and practitioners to understand the implications of different SOC options and how to build and operate a successful SOC that meets their business needs and achieves goal of protecting digital assets. The book starts with an introduction to SOC and then builds on basic concepts to achieve excellence in building and operating a modern SOC. The objective is to provide the reader a complete guide, starting from building business case, acquiring needed technologies, hiring and training people for SOC operations, and building a governance model for measuring success and for continuous improvement.

1.1   What is a Security Operations Center (SOC)?

A Security Operations Center (SOC) is typically an organization inside a business that is responsible for protecting critical business assets by continuously monitoring emerging threats, collect notable security events, analyzing and prioritizing these events, and responding to security incidents.

SANS institute defines SOC as:

"A combination of people, processes and technology protecting the information systems of an organization through: proactive design and configuration, ongoing monitoring of system state, detection of unintended actions or undesirable state, and minimizing damage from unwanted effects." [10]

3

Typically a SOC consists of components as shown in Figure 1.1, with technology stack at the core, data and threat intelligence feeding into the technology stack, and wrapped with people, processes, and a governance model:

1. **People** with different levels of expertise in diverse areas including networking, operating systems, applications, operations management, scripting, Python, vulnerability management, incident handling, forensics and others.

2. Defined **processes** for tasks under the scope of SOC. While there are many SOC processes, effective incident detection and incident management is a key process for success of every SOC. A SOC may also rely on other IT systems/processes like asset management, change management, patch management etc.

3. **Technology Stack** for collecting log and other types of telemetry data, storing data, and processing/analyzing data. Main technologies used in SOC include Security Information and Event Management (SIEM) tool, log collection, network sensing, ticket/incident management, forensic tools, and vulnerability management tools.

4. **SOC Governance** structure that enables SOC management and continuous improvement while ensuring the business objectives of SOC are achieved.

5. Carefully selected **Data Sources** provide high value in threat detection. People need to be careful and selective in determining the type and amount of data that is fed into the technology stack. More is not always better!

6. **Threat Intelligence** is a must for the success of any modern SOC. It helps in proactive threat hunting and helps in automation, responding to threats at machine speed.

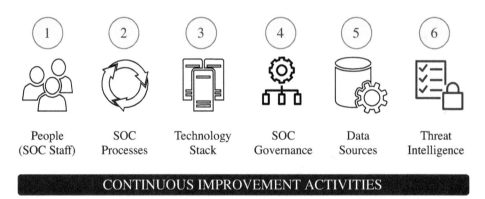

Figure 1.1: Ingredients of a successful Security Operations Center

While these ingredients are necessary to build a successful SOC, continuous improvement activities are absolutely necessary to keep SOC effective and continuously deliver value. Continuous improvements require that SOC managers look for opportunities of improvement in all of these areas including training of SOC staff.

As we discuss later in this book, many operating models are used in industry depending upon needs of a particular organization.

> While building a SOC, you don't necessarily need to have all of the SOC components in-house. You can make business decisions about what to keep in-house and where to get help from your security partners/vendors.

1.1.1 What is a Modern SOC?

A modern SOC goes beyond dealing with detection of known threat and responding to incidents. It not only supports emerging technologies but also uses these technologies to improve SOC performance. A modern SOC implements all or a subset of the following:

- Includes physical security in the scope

- Integrate monitoring of Operational Technologies

- Use data analytics and machine learning for detection of previously unknown threat

- Subscribe to threat intelligence and potentially use a *Threat Intelligence Platform* or *TIP*

- Automate routine tasks for improving efficiency and speed of incident handling

- Close collaboration with broader IT teams as well as business leadership

- Build a learning culture for SOC staff to be continuously up-to-date about emerging threats

- Share knowledge and intelligence both inside the organization as well as with trusted industry forums and partners

- Integrates threat detection for emerging technologies

- Contributes to developing policies and standards to make SOC integration as part of project management and software delivery lifecycle

With the increased focus on protection of data and critical systems, skills development to manage a SOC are also becoming more and more challenging. A breadth of knowledge in many different areas is required to be an effective SOC analyst.

1.1.2 SOC Functions

A SOC is part of an overall risk management program and serves some basic functions as listed below and shown in Figure 1.2.

- Collect and manage logs as well as other useful telemetry data

- Gather intelligence on threat actors, attack methods, and indicators of compromise

- Analyze available data and create/rank alerts based upon risk to the organization

- Promptly respond to security incidents and minimize impact of incidents on business

To keep focus on success of core business and to optimize cost, many organizations outsource some or all of these functions to security vendors. Only very few businesses opt to completely manage an in-house SOC.

1.2 Purpose: Why Build SOC?

Before you embark on the journey of building a SOC, establish the purpose of SOC and have the business leadership agree on it. The *purpose* must be business driven instead of technology driven. The purpose must answer the question: *Why do you really want to build a SOC?* The answer could be very different depending on the type of an organization. For example, a manufacturing corporation may need to ensure safe/smooth operation of plants, protecting intellectual property and manufacturing processes. On the other hand, primary purpose of a

Figure 1.2: SOC Functions

bank may be protecting consumer data and avoid financial fraud. A hospital may be worried about malware, ransomware, or protection against exploitation of medical equipment.

Some of the other areas of consideration are:

- Better risk management

- Fulfill compliance needs

- Business enablement

- Gain competitive advantage

In any case, establishing a clear purpose of SOC will help you narrow the focus of SOC, and better utilize investments.

1.3   SOC Business Models

There are three main business models for SOC, although there are number of variations within each of these models. These models are summarized below.

1.3.1   In-House SOC

A completely in-house SOC is where an organization fully owns and manages operations of SOC. The organizations owns the technology and processes as well as hires people to operate the SOC. This is usually an expensive proposition and very few organizations have a business case to build and operate an in-house SOC. The size of the SOC may vary significantly depending upon the size of the organization and the scope.

1.3.2 Completely Outsourced SOC

Many organizations opt to engage a *Managed Security Services Provider* (MSSP) to build and operate SOC on behalf of the company. Sometimes it is also known as *"SOC as a service"* model . A major objective of this model is to benefit from experience of service providers, benefit from their established processes and get access to ongoing threat intelligence. Some companies buy or subscribe their own technology stack while others use technology from the service provider.

Typically, the organization still owns remediation tasks and participates in incident response in a completely outsourced SOC model.

1.3.3 Partially Outsourced SOC

In a partially outsourced SOC, some processes and technologies are owned by the organization while others are managed by a service provider (MSSP). A common example is outsourcing forensics and log analytics while keeping ownership of incident response and remediation. However, there are large number of variations in this model depending upon which components of a SOC you would like to outsource and which ones to keep in-house.

1.4 What it Takes to Build a SOC?

Building an in-house SOC is a major undertaking and it is much more than just buying and installing software tools. A SOC is a combination of a clear business purpose, a technology stack, processes, governance structure, hiring and continuously training people, and maintaining executive support. Please keep the following in mind when you are embarking on a journey to build a SOC:

- You should always start with a clear business purpose and desired outcome for a SOC

- Defining clear scope is very crucial and most people stumble in the beginning by not doing so.

- Proper planning for SOC implementation can save significant trouble later in the SOC lifecycle

- It may take more than a year (may be 2-3 years) to have a completely functional SOC

- It is a significant financial undertaking and executive support is necessary

- SOC needs continuous improvement, so you have to plan for budget to support improvement tasks in overall operational cost

- Building SOC is much more than just technology or implementing a SIEM platform

- It would be a mistake to try to build all capabilities in-house. For example, you may need some capabilities very infrequently (e.g. deep forensic expertise). A prudent approach is to contract with your partners/vendors for some tasks that don't need day-to-day work.

A successful SOC will test your tenacity, persistence, coalition building skills, and getting things done through influence rather than authority as you have to work with broader IT teams.

1.5 SOC Implementation: Incremental or Big Bang?

Should one make a big comprehensive plan for implementing SOC in one go using waterfall methodology, or use agile concepts to make improvements over time? Arguments can be made in both ways, but you should consider that building SOC is usually a multi-year project. A big bang approach can be a disaster in some situations whereas an incremental approach can help you learn and fine tune your strategy over a period of time by taking smaller steps. I am always for building a complete and multi-year strategy but starting with a small scope.

You should always prioritize and divide your SOC roadmap into three to six months long sub-projects (the smaller, the better). Consider the most important aspects that need to be implemented in these phases to build scope of your sub-projects. These aspects may fall into multiple categories like the following:

- *Technical aspects* such as log sources that need to be added to the scope, or types of use cases[1] that need to be created.

- *Organizational aspects* may matter in larger and diversified organizations. For example, you may want to include or exclude some business units from SOC scope for a particular sub-project.

- *Regional* scope in the case of global organizations is quite important. In the initial phases of SOC implementation, my suggestion is to focus on one region or country and then bring other regions under SOC scope. This will also help you deal with regional and country-specific laws and compliance requirements gradually.

- *Single or Multiple SOC* implementations are a consideration in the case of global organizations where it could be important to keep data in certain regions.

You may have other categories specific to your organization and how you plan to use SOC for risk mitigation. The idea is to create a structured approach for dividing the task of SOC implementing into 6-12 phases over a three year period.

1.5.1 Single Site or Multi-Site

Some large organizations may decide to start with a single SOC, learn and fine tune their approach, and then create regional or business unit SOC separately. There may be business reasons from budgeting perspective. A common organizational reason is that IT and Security responsibilities for different business units are not under one management.

Another reason for multi-site SOC is 24x7x365 operations where organizations build multiple SOC in follow-the-sun model. I will cover multiple SOC implications later in the book in detail from the perspective of hiring people and scheduling.

1.5.2 Business Unit Coverage

Large size organizations have multiple business units that may belong to completely different industry sectors. To properly manage risk, they may decide to build SOC initially with a limited scope covering only high-risk business units. Once they have covered the high risk areas, then they may decide to add more business units in a gradual manner.

1.6 SOC Lifecycle Phases

Building SOC is not a one-time activity but a continuous journey. As mentioned earlier, a good practiced is to start small. Plan, design, implement, and operationalize the initial phase. Learn from SOC operations and improve scope/plan of next phases based upon your experience.

---

[1] A use case is a specific situation that the SOC technology will be configured to detect. For example, ransomware detection or insider threat detection.

> In many cases multiple phases of SOC will be in progress at any given time. For example, you may be testing SOC operations from phase 1 while working on scope and planning for phase 2. This increases complexity and need for oversight.

Typical SOC lifecycle is shown in Figure 1.3.

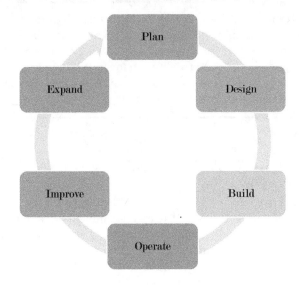

Figure 1.3: SOC Lifecycle Phases

Following is a brief summary of activities for each phase.

1. **Plan** phase is about defining a SOC mission, scope, building business case, getting executive sponsorship, budget approvals, and defining business outcomes.

2. **Design** phase includes making decisions about technology stack, locations, logistics, network and connectivity, log sources, hiring people, defining processes, building partnerships with IT teams and so on.

3. **Build** phase is all about implementing your design, fine tuning few things as you discover new/additional options that you may not have considered in design phase, start collecting logs, creating use cases and testing alerts.

4. **Operate** phase starts when you have built and tested SOC technology as well as processes and move to the steady state processes. Here you will schedule personnel, respond to alerts, create reports, use metrics and measure performance of your SOC.

5. **Improve** phase is related to standardizing process, fine tuning technology stack, creating new use cases, automate routine tasks. This is all about getting the best out of SOC investment. The improve phases starts right after the operations and continues in parallel.

6. **Expand** phase is part of multi-phase part of SOC where you start small initially. For example, you may have only one business unit in the initial scope or may have a subset of log sources in the beginning. Once you have built some experience, then you will expand SOC to include additional areas of IT organization or add more business units, or going from local to global.

As you may have realized by now, SOC lifecycle goes into a circle. When you start expanding SOC in the *Expand* phase, you will get back to the planning and design and repeat the cycle. While the initial SOC implementation is a two-three years long project, continuous improvement and automation is an ongoing activity.

What about program management?

One question to consider: is there any value in having program management involvement over the multi-year approach? Since there are multiple phases occurring, perhaps simultaneously, an experienced program manager can better oversee budgets, timing, resources (technology, personnel) as well as manage governance reports for all stakeholders. Depending upon size and scope of the SOC project, a program management approach may be necessary but not always required.

1.7   Who are the Stakeholders?

One may tend to think that information security is the largest, if not the only, stakeholder in setting up a SOC. However, that is hardly the case for numerous reasons. Not only do most of the IT teams play their role in building and operating SOC, non-IT teams like human resources, finance, legal, and public relations teams also need to be part of a comprehensive SOC strategy. Following is a short description of some of these stakeholders. More will be discussed later in this book.

- **The Network** teams play an important role. They are responsible for enabling SOC connectivity, segmenting SOC from the rest of the network, providing access to key data points like Netflows and full packet capture, and ensure that proper network capacity exists for collecting log data.

- **Server Infrastructure** teams not only provide support for key system in SOC but are also crucial to collect system logs, authentication data from identity and access management systems, among many other support items.

- **Human Resource** department plays key role in finding the right people for SOC staff, their training and retention.

- **CFO** and finance teams approve budget and embed SOC in corporate risk management strategy. Without their support, realizing SOC budget could be a daunting task.

- **The Legal** teams provide support and cover for SOC activities that may result in legal issues (both internal and external) as a result of data leakages and breaches. Legal teams also play their role in negotiation contracts with MSSP and other technology providers.

- **Compliance** teams will rely on SOC to partially meet your organization's compliance needs. For example, PCI, HIPAA and other standards require log collection and threat detection which is a common function of SOC.

Building a coalition of internal teams and including them in SOC planning is, thus, crucial for your success. The sooner you start engaging them in a proactive manner, the better it is. Considering an inclusive governance board for SOC is always a great idea.

1.8 SOC Operations Time

Do you want to run Security Operations Center during the working hours, day time or round the clock? Your adversaries definitely don't follow your work hours, so you may want to think about your approach!

- **Business Hours** operation may include 8 AM to 5 PM.

- **24x7x365** operations, as the name shows, is for round the clock coverage.

- **Follow-the-Sun** model is still 24x7x365 operation but in this case you have multiple SOCs across the globe such that each individual SOC works only in the business hours of their respective region. However, when combined together, the SOC offers a complete 24x7x365 coverage.

More of this will be covered under section 2.7

1.9 SOC Stakeholders' Perspective

When building SOC business case, be mindful that people have different perspectives about SOC goals and objectives. Put yourself in the shows of the following roles and think how SOC will bring *value* to each of them.

- Business Executives

- Information Security Leaders

- Security practitioners

- Other IT teams including but not limited to IT, Network, Applications, Desktop and so on

There should be something for each team in the SOC plan. A CISO must also build a cross functional SOC governance committee as discussed later in this book.

1.10 Threat Modeling

Threat modeling is crucial task for planning and building a successful SOC. While this book is not intended to be a text on threat modeling, in simple words think about threat modeling as a practice to understand your adversaries, their methods to attack your organization, how you will identify the attacks and respond to these attacks. Threat modeling will help you define scope, determine interesting log sources, select appropriate tools and technologies and many other aspects to make SOC successful.

Many texts and online resources are available for threat modeling and my advice is to make it a standard practice to model and remodel threats. In the absence of proper threat modeling, you will end up wasting significant time, money and energy in collecting irrelevant logs and investigating events that don't matter much. Threat modeling will also help you in creating appropriate use cases and filtering out noise.

1.11 Chapter Summary and Recommendations

Building a security operations center is a serious undertaking. It is prudent to start with collecting information, evaluating options and defining purpose of a SOC. It is crucial to answer a fundamental question: Why do you want to build a SOC? Once you have that question answered, then you can work on the following to build your understanding of different options:

- SOC business models (in-house, outsources, hybrid)

- SOC operating models (business hours or 24x7x365, follow-the-sun, single or multiple SOC)

- Understanding SOC lifecycle

- Phased approaches

- Understanding stakeholders

- Executive sponsorship

- Who could be part of SOC governance team?

- Building a business case

- Implementation plan

- Acquiring technologies

- Hiring and staffing

A well-thought out approach about the above will provide the base for a successful development of business case followed by the design and implementation.

"A business case captures the reasoning for initiating a project or task. It is often presented in a well-structured written document, but may also sometimes come in the form of a short verbal argument or presentation. The logic of the business case is that, whenever resources such as money or effort are consumed, they should be in support of a specific business need."

The Free Dictionary (tfd.com)

2

SOC Business Case Development

Building a security operations center (SOC) is a significant undertaking. In additional to personal commitment, it requires significant investment of money, time and other resources. Like any other project, it should always start with building a compelling business case. A typical business case includes many sections as outlined later in this chapter, however, it should always start with answering this fundamental question: Why do you want to build a SOC? As it takes some time and many iterations to build a sound business case, you should start working on it quite early. You can start with an outline of your business case using a template in section 2.15 and then modify as needed. As you work on building the business case, it is a good idea to get input from other business leaders in your organization as well as few peers you trust the most.

While building the business case for SOC, you should consider the following sections:

- Industry analysis

- Mission and goals

- SOC Scope

- Tools and technologies

- SOC location and space needs

- Staff requirements and management structure

- SOC operational plan

- Implementation phases

- Financial analysis

- SOC governance model

- Continuous improvement plan

A business case is a way to perform your due diligence and explore different options to achieve business goals. It is also a tool to get support, approval and funding for building SOC. This chapter provides guidance and a template for building SOC business case and help you get started.

2.1 Who is the Audience and Stakeholders?

Understanding the audience of SOC business case is key to proactively address their concerns, answer their questions, and getting the plan approved. Typically there are multiple groups of audience for your business case. You have to speak to all of them, although in different parts of your business case. Some of these groups are listed below.

- **Executive Management** - this includes people who are ultimately responsible for approving the budget. They need to understand business outcomes of SOC, financial analysis, return on investment, risk reduction, and which problem the SOC solves. The business case should clearly show why they should spend money on SOC and not on other competing projects. Remember, funds are always limited and executive management always have to pick projects based upon the *value* each project brings to the business and shareholders. For example:

  - CFO - Will write a check for the SOC and will expect some return on investment and reduction in risk.

  - CIO - Will will support SOC activities through extended IT teams and would be interested in understanding how SOC brings efficiency to operations, among other things.

  - Chief Legal Officer - Cover legal aspects of SOC when needed.

  Depending upon your particular organization, consider the C-level leadership and include how SOC project takes care of their interests.

- **Middle Management** - These are typically director level people who are looking for interests of their own departments and potentially competing with you for budget of their own projects. If you are able to tie the SOC objectives with some of their objectives, you will increase chances of success of getting their support. For example, if SOC can provide analytics capability that improves time to troubleshoot IT incidents, you can build alliance with your internal server or network teams.

- **Managers and IT Architects** - They have interest in how SOC will impact their daily life either positively or negatively. Will it make their lives easy or will it create extra work for them? Here you have to focus on making their work easy in terms providing timely information and incident resolution. You definitely want to avoid projecting SOC as something that can increase workload for other IT teams.

Each of these audience are looking for different things in the business case that caters to their specific needs and interests. You should strive to provide something for all stakeholders in your business case as much as possible.

2.2 Why Build SOC?

This is the most important and most crucial question to answer, but it must be answered. Unless you find a great answer, it would be a challenge to market the SOC internally and get funding. You will be challenged with comments like why we have to do it? Can't we live without it? Do other companies of our size and industry run SOC? How will it help business? And so on.

You have to bring all of your expertise together to find the best answer to this question: be a professor, a marketer, a business savvy professional, a financial analyst, a risk manager, and a visionary. You can start collecting all reasons why a SOC is needed and then create your elevator pitch based upon what is the most important for your audience.

Consider ideas like the following:

- Risk Management?

- Compliance?

- Business Enablement?

- Competitive Advantage?

- Other reasons?

If you are working in a technology company, may be *business enablement* and *competitive advantage* are the most important aspects of your pitch. If you are in financial sector, overall *risk management* is always a concern.

Why is it important to answer the *why* question

Note that answering this question is not only necessary to create your elevator pitch, it is extremely important for youself and the security team as well. This will provide a common vision to all stakeholders and will guide you through the scoping and planning phases.[39]

A research on why similar organizations in your industry have build SOC will also help.

> In some cases, highlighting cost of *not building a SOC* can also be very useful for your audience to understand the importance of SOC.

2.3 Building a Story

A compelling story adds significant impact to any business case. While discussion in section 2.2 will help you create your elevator pitch, the story can be placed in the beginning of the business case document. A simple story can be built on the following steps:

1. *Where are we right now?* - Describe the current industry landscape, how security operations are managed within your organization, gaps, and risks.

2. *How the future looks like?* - Explain the future state and paint a compelling picture for your audience.

3. *Why we need to get there?* - Utilize your thought process for answering the *Why* question in section 2.2.

4. *How do we get there?* - Describe different options to get to the future state and the reason why you are choosing a particular path.

> Building a story is an essential part of influencing stake holders where they understand what the future looks like and become enthusiastic in joining you on a journey.

2.4   Business Case Sections

Depending upon your company culture, you may have a business case only few pages long or it may span 10-15 pages. Some organizations have specific templates for building business cases. The remainder of this chapter highlights some sections that I would recommend for your SOC business case development.

> Many times you would think that you are building business case for others. However, in my view developing a business case is beneficial for you more than anyone else. It gives you an opportunity to think deeply about your goals and the challenges you may face in this endeavor. So more than anything else, do it for yourself.

2.5   SOC Mission

Mission statement should be short and define clearly the purpose of SOC, incorporate the notion of *SOC customers*[1], what service would it provide and how these services will benefit SOC customers. If your mission statement is more than two sentences long, you should trim it down. A mission statement is something that you would memorize, use as a poster, and make it your video screen wallpaper. This is the statement that you will continuously remind people, so it better be awesome!

2.6   SOC Goals

The goals should have a short list of objectives that you would like to achieve. I would suggest making goal list between three to five points. If you have too many goals, you may lose focus and dilute the message. Following are some examples of the goals and considerations that you may want to include but there could be others, more relevant to your organization.

- Goals related to revenue and cost

- Risk management goals

- Operational efficiency and speedy incident detection/response

- Corporate business goals and how SOC goals align with those

While defining SOC goals, keep in mind your audience. This is crucial part of your business plan. Setting ambiguous goals, or the ones that can't be measured or achievable, or the ones that are not relevant to your organization, will be a mistake. Many times people make mistake of setting lofty goals and use information security terminology that others are not able to understand.

Using SMART (Specific, Measurable, Attainable, Realistic, and Time-bound) [45] method of setting goals is a good starting point. However, make sure that each goal you set is a *good idea* in the first place. You should go through multiple iterations of your goal list. Take feedback from other security professionals and use simple terms that people outside security can easily understand.

Once the information security team feels good about the list, take feedback from few key members of broader IT team who you trust. Make further iterations based upon their feedback.

---

[1]Customer is used as a generic term to define consumers of the SOC services. The customers may include internal IT operations, network, helpdesk, and others

Many SOC projects are multi-year long. It is a good idea to align your goal with each phase of the project. This will also help define scope of the project.

2.7 Defining SOC Scope

While defining SOC mission and goals are key starting points, defining SOC scope is crucial to manage the overall SOC project and break a large multi-year project into smaller phases. You can further break each phase into milestones. This also helps in managing cost and simplify implementation. My suggestion is to divide a SOC project over multiple phases, each of which should be about six months long. Following are some key areas to consider when defining the scope of each phase.

2.7.1 SCOPE: Log Sources

Log sources vary widely, starting from security device logs, network components, applications, servers, Cloud and many others. Collecting logs also needs significant investment in log storage and processing infrastructure. You want to prioritize log sources that bring the most value from security monitoring perspective. For these reasons, you should start with a small subset of log sources and expand the scope of log collection over time (in future phases of the project). While defining the scope of log collection for each phase, you can consider the following:

- Value of particular log source for identifying security events and detecting noticeable incidents.

- How a particular log source can help in incident investigations.

- Amount of log data that you can handle, both from analytics and storage perspectives.

- Compliance *needs and requirements* that a particular log source fulfills.

- Ease of collecting log data from a particular source.

Typically, you should start with logs coming from security devices (firewalls, IDS, content filtering and proxy servers, identity management systems, VPN concentrators, end-point detection and response systems, etc). The second preference may be server operating systems and public facing web server logs. Then you can move to applications, and so on. There is no prescribed order and you should define your own scope based upon your particular situation and which systems play a key role inside your organization.

With most of the organizations moving to Cloud, collecting logs from Cloud service providers like AWS, Azure, Google and others could become a priority for some organizations. Additionally, if you are using a Cloud Access Security Broker (CASB), collecting logs from CASB system in the initial phases of SOC implementation will also be a good idea.

For some manufacturing organizations, logs from IoT devices and operational technologies could provide significant value. Auto manufacturers could be interested in logs from connected vehicles.

You can also use threat modeling techniques to identify critical log sources and prioritize these accordingly.

2.7.2 SCOPE: Time of Day

Although everybody would like to have a 24x7x365 SOC but that is not always possible due to different constraints. An 8x5 (8 AM to 5 PM) or single-shift SOC may be a good starting point for many organizations, at least in the initial phases of SOC implementation. Once the initial phase is complete, you may want to add a second shift before going to a full 24x7x365 operation. Global organizations may also start with a single centralized SOC in one region and then use follow-the-sun model to achieve 24x7x365 coverage.

2.7.3   SCOPE: Business Units

Large organizations have multiple business units and all of these business units don't need to be under SOC scope, or at least not in the first phase. While each organization may have a different criteria to identify which business unites to cover, some considerations may include:

- Criticality of a business unit for the organization.

- Type of data and privacy requirements.

- Compliance needs and local rules/regulations.

- Risk to brand as a result of large-scale security incident.

Selection of business units may also be phased approach.

2.7.4   SCOPE: Geographical Locations

Multinational organizations may decide SOC scope based upon preference of specific geographic locations, among other criteria.

2.7.5   SCOPE: Emerging Technologies

Fast emergence of new technologies including Internet of Things (IoT), blockchains, autonomous vehicles, drones, and others is also impacting security business. While this may not be the case for some, others may deem these technologies as business critical based upon their impact. Following are some technologies that you may want to cover in different phases of a SOC project.

- Machine Learning (ML), deep learning and other artificial intelligence related technologies.

- Internet of Things or IoT, collecting data from IoT devices, IoT botnets, identities and other aspects of IoT.

- Operational Technologies or OT that cover factories, industrial controls, SCADA systems.

- BlockChain

- Drones

- Autonomous vehicles

- Migration to Cloud

Your business is potentially a provider or consumer of at least some of these technologies. You may also be interested in bringing these under SOC scope because you may be a service provider. In any case, threats to these and other emerging technologies are only going to grow as their deployment and use grows.

Following are few other areas to consider for SOC scope:

- **Incident Handling** - Demarcation of where incident response will be handed over to other IT/OT/Physical security teams and which parts will be covered by the SOC staff. This will also help in determination of who needs access to incident management application and be part of incident response team.

- **Incident Handling Support** - Which part of incidents will be outsourced to third parties, if any. For example, if the SOC does not include building in-depth forensic capability, it can be outsourced to a third party for major incidents.

- **Managing SOC IT Infrastructure** - SOC team manages security applications including SIEM and security tools. However, IT infrastructure is needed to run these applications and tools. Decide who will manage network, storage, and server Operating System for SOC IT infrastructure. Who approves processes for incident handling when people outside SOC are involved in the incident response activities?

- **Connection with Outside Parties** - When outside parties like press, communication, law enforcement are engaged, decide who will establish relationships with these outside parties and manage communications with them.

- **Other Data Collection Scope** – Decide and define the scope of data collections other than logs, including netflows, threat intelligence, physical security and so on. If Cloud environment is in the scope, what data can be collected from the Cloud Service Providers (CSP)?

- **Vulnerability Management** - Who manages critical vulnerabilities, from scanning to prioritization to patching?

- **Threat Intelligence Gathering and Use** - How threat intelligence will be gathered and utilized (internal or outsourced/purchased)?

- **Processes** - Define which processes will be part of SOC and which will be excluded. For example, is SOC responsible of education and awareness, pen testing, or patching? Depending upon organizational structure, these and other security operational processes may be part of SOC or outside of its scope.

- **Compliance** - What role SOC has in achieving and maintaining compliance with government and/or industry regulations. Also, does the SOC itself have to comply with any standards or regulations?

2.8 Tools and Technologies

A major cost element of SOC business case is purchase of software/hardware tools and services. Other than log collection infrastructure, SIEM is a primary tool that almost all SOC implementations will use. Fortunately many Cloud based options are available where you can avoid capital expense on these technologies. Once again a phased approach could be very useful to kickstart your project such that you are making capital expenses on a gradual basis.

Following is a list of tools to consider for purchase at different stages of SOC implementation plan:

- Log collection and analysis tools, including SIEM.

- Vulnerability scanning and penetration testing.

- Incident lifecycle management and ticketing.

- Forensic and evidence collection.

- Threat intelligence platform.

In addition to core tools and technologies, you may have to rely on other IT teams for managing server infrastructure for SOC, desktops and laptops used by SOC analysts, networking gear, and other common IT services.

> Explore if any open source tools and technologies will be a good fit for your SOC implementation.

2.9   SOC Operations Management

From a day to day operations management perspective, there are three basic models that you can choose from:

- **Internal Management** - Your organization manages all SOC operations internally with your technology, by your people and using your own processes.

- **MSSP Management** - A Managed Security Services Provider (MSSP) that manages SOC operations with their own tools and processes while you collaborate with the MSSP for incident management and remediation.

- **Hybrid Management** - This is where you manage SOC but outsource some parts where you don't have or don't want to build internal capability for various reasons. For example, you may want to outsource forensics if this is done rarely and does not justify full time employees.

The operations management is a crucial decision and should not be taken lightly. In some cases it would make sense to keep the operations in-house whereas in other cases outsourcing may make sense. When building business case, make sure your focus on the *business outcomes instead of owning a technology*. The ultimate decision may also include considerations for compliance needs.

2.10   Staffing Needs

Main SOC staffing needs depend upon few key decisions like the following:

- Number of shifts, whether SOC is 8x5 or 24x7.

- SOC functions kept in-house or outsourced.

- Using internal infrastructure for SIEM or use a Cloud service.

You should consider number of people required for 24x7x365 SOC keeping in view vacation time, people getting sick or leaving company, weekends, and so on. Although collaboration with other IT and network teams can reduce staffing needs, the business case should not bet on that aspect as the SOC needs to stand and operate on its own.

Some research has shown that staffing needs could also be a factor of size of your organizations [10].

2.11   SOC Logistics

Although it may seem trivial, you should not forget common logistics for building SOC. These include but not limited to the following:

- Location, rooms

- Furniture and lighting

- Desktops and laptops needed for staff

- Secure cabinets and other logistics for storage of evidence

- HVAC and environmental safety [44]

- Any TV screens and signal to display weather, breaking news etc.

In the business plan, include these factors and make them part of financial analysis and budget requirements.

2.12   Budget and Financial Analysis

This section is the most crucial for your CFO and people who will approve the budget[2]. Some key aspects to consider and make your financial analysis more compelling may include:

- Take a phased approach and spread your budget over a period of time. Start small and then expand over 2-3 years, if you have the flexibility.

- Ensure projecting return from SOC investments. The return may not always be in terms of money but could be in terms of risk reduction and efficiency. Try to quantify, but if you can't then define outcomes qualitatively.

- Think about taking advantage of existing technologies and open source tools.

- Separate capital costs from operational costs. Don't forget to increase operational cost on yearly basis.

- Don't forget amortization and depreciation of capital goods.

- Include costs for any professional services for initial implementation.

Figure 2.1 shows a sample calculation for SOC budget. However, it is very simple and your calculations may be more complicated, taking into account multiple phases.

The finance people will pay attention to the terminology, so make sure you use the right financial terms and keywords they would be looking for.

2.13   SOC Governance Model

The SOC governance model is part of the overall security program governance. You should always form a governance committee and include key stakeholders in the committee to create governance framework. The committee is responsible for creating and approving SOC policies and processes, approve any changes to the existing policies and processes, and provide oversight to SOC activities. Figure 2.2 shows potential members of a SOC governance committee and its responsibilities.

Please note that the governance committee is responsible for delegating authority to SOC for taking certain actions and provide an oversight to ensure that SOC operations teams is using the authorization properly.

---

[2]You can use a simple budget calculator spreadsheet from my blog site http://rafeeqrehman.com

Budget for Setting up SOC

SOC Budget Calculator Version 1, December 2016

Annual Personnel Cost Estimates

This is an estimate for 24x7 SOC with three shifts. Annual costs and number of analysts can change based upon your needs.

Job Item	Quantity	Individual Annual Cost	Total Annual Cost
Tier 1 Analysts	5	$80,000.00	$400,000.00
Tier 2 Analysts	3	$100,000.00	$300,000.00
Tier 3 Analysts/Threat Hunters	2	$120,000.00	$240,000.00
Forensic Specialist	1	$130,000.00	$130,000.00
Malware Engineer	1	$120,000.00	$120,000.00
SOC Manager	1	$140,000.00	$140,000.00
		Total Annual Cost:	**$1,330,000.00**

Capital Cost Estimates

Change the following costs depnding upon your own estimates. Consider these numbers as placeholder only.

Description	Quantity	Item Cost	Total Cost
SIEM Solution	1	$200,000.00	$200,000.00
Server Hardware	3	$100,000.00	$300,000.00
Laptops	13	$1,500.00	$19,500.00
Forensic Software	1	$40,000.00	$40,000.00
Secure Cabinets/Locks	1	$5,000.00	$5,000.00
Forensic Image Storage	1	$10,000.00	$10,000.00
Log Storage and backup	1	$200,000.00	$200,000.00
Office, Furniture, etc	1	$200,000.00	$200,000.00
Miscellaneous	1	$200,000.00	$200,000.00
Professional Consulting/design/setup	1	$100,000.00	$100,000.00
	Total Technology Capital Cost:		**$1,274,500.00**

Annual Recurring Cost Estimates

Everything below is an estimate. Change based upon discussion with vendors

Description	Quantity	Item Cost	Total Cost
Depreciation of office equipment			$0.00
Software/Hardware Maintenenace			$0.00
Staff Training, Skills update	13	5000	$65,000.00
IR Exercises	4	3000	$12,000.00
Threat Intelligence Feeds	1	10000	$10,000.00
Vulnerability Scanning (Network)	1	$40,000.00	$40,000.00
Vulnerability Scanning (Applications)	1	$30,000.00	$30,000.00
		Total Annual Cost:	**$157,000.00**

Grand Total

Following are estimated grand total costs (capital and annual recurring).

Grand total capital cost of establishing SOC:	**$1,274,500.00**
Grand total annual recurring cost for SOC:	**$1,487,000.00**

Figure 2.1: SOC Budget Calculator

The governance committee should also perform regular audits of SOC operations, define/approve performance metrics, and review SOC performance on regular basis. It is also responsible to coordinate SOC improvement activities with broader IT teams and ensure that continuous improvement to SOC technologies and processes takes place. The committee may also require creation and review of annual reports. At the same time, the committee should also ensure

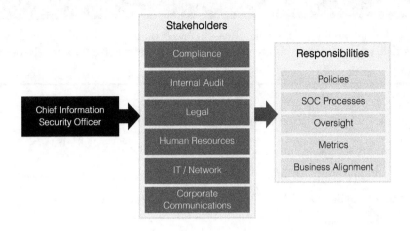

Figure 2.2: SOC governance committee and its responsibilities

that the oversight burden is minimal and kept in check.

While creating business case, it is a good idea to investigate potential candidates for the governance committee, their roles, and the value they will bring to the committee. You don't want to create a large group that may complicate the decision making process. At the same time, you don't want to miss a key stakeholder either. Also, make sure that members of the committee have appropriate authority to make decisions.

2.14 Risk Analysis

This may be a rather smaller section in your business case. You can address risk of building a SOC vs. risk of not building a SOC while keeping in view the following key areas:

- *Compliance Risk* - How this initiative will effect compliance needs?

- *Financial Risk* - Improvement in financial risk because SOC can lower probability of breaches or lower the impact of a breach. At the same time risk of losing money if the project fails.

- *Technology Change* - What if technology acquired for the project becomes obsolete or does not meet the needs of changing threat landscape? How can you lower this risk by using Cloud technology or use a managed security services provider who takes the ownership of technology risk?

- *Talent Retention* - For running SOC, you need to attract and retain qualified people. How would you manage risk of trained people leaving the organization?

- *Infrastructure Risk* - The underlying IT infrastructure risks are assumed with SOC. As an example, how would you plan for business continuity and disaster recovery.

Why risk analysis is important?

A good risk analysis in your business case shows your due diligence in understanding business risk, your plan to mitigate or minimize risk, and the best approach to providing resilience.

2.15   SOC Business Case Template

Following are major sections of a SOC business case template.

1. Introduction and industry analysis

2. Definition of business problem

3. SOC mission and goals

4. SOC scope

5. Tools and technologies

6. Location and space needs

7. Staffing requirements

8. Operational plan

   - Governance structure

   - Policies and procedures

9. Implementation phases and milestones

   - Year 1 plan

     - **Business case development and approval**

     - **Technology procurement**

     - **Staffing**

     - **Initial SIEM implementation**

     - **Log sources** - Security logs

     - **Time coverage**

     - **Business Unites**

     - **Covered technologies**

     - **Tools and Technologies**

     - **Others**

   - Year 2 plan

     - **Log Sources** - Security Logs

     - **Time coverage**

     - **Business Unites**

     - **Covered technologies**

- **Tools and Technologies**

- **Additional SIEM use cases development**

- **Others**

- Year 3 plan

  - **Log Sources** - Security Logs

  - **Time coverage**

  - **Business Unites**

  - **Covered technologies**

  - **Tools and Technologies**

  - **Additional SIEM use cases development**

  - **Others**

10. SOC financial analysis

11. Risk Analysis

12. Summary and conclusions

Feel free to modify this template based upon your own needs as all sections of this template may not be applicable in smaller organizations.

2.16 Chapter Summary and Recommendations

Business case is a key tool for success of a SOC project. A thoughtful approach to developing business case takes time and collaboration among stakeholders. It also helps building relationships inside broader technology teams that become crucial in the later parts of implementation. While building SOC business case, consider the following:

- An exceptional business case is not only necessary to get approval and funding, it is also important for you to better plan for the SOC project.

- You have to wear multiple hats to build the business case, be open and transparent, and get input from different stakeholders.

- Going to management for budget without due diligence and without building a business case is a mistake.

- Building a business case without getting feedback from your superiors about corporate business strategy and lack of aligning SOC with the overall strategy is another common mistake.

- I highly recommend spending good amount of time on building SOC mission and goals and answering the *why* questions.

- Use template provided in section 2.15 as a starting point but modify it based upon your needs.

- Use diagrams in the business case, such as organizational chart, governance committee, etc.

- Always split business plan in multiple phases so that you don't have to request a very large budget at one time.

- A sound financial analysis is crucial for the business plan. *Don't minimize* required funding as you may have to go back for extra money later on.

—*Torture the data, and it will con-
fess to anything.*

Ronald Coase

*You can have data without infor-
mation, but you cannot have information without data.*

Daniel Keys

3

Logs and Other Data Sources

Logs are a primary and key telemetry data source and that is one of the reasons almost all security standards and frameworks (NIST, ISO, PCI, and others) emphasize collection, storage, and analysis of log data as one of the key component of a security program. Collecting, correlating, and analyzing logs is a fundamental function of any SOC implementation. Logs also provide valuable information and evidence to meet many compliance needs.

However, as we know, some log sources provide much more value to security programs and threat detection compared to others. So while you can collect, store and process all data you want, an evaluation of the true value a particular log data source can help create a more cost-effective and focused strategy.

A phased approach for log management is always prudent where you start with important, more valuable log sources first and then add additional log data over time as your program matures.

Traditional log collection, either using Syslog protocol or monitoring log files, has worked for quite some time. With ever faster transition newer technologies are bringing challenges to older log collection methods. With transition to Cloud based technologies, newer log data may come from sources like SàaS[1] applications, Cloud application platforms, server-less applications, IoT devices, operational technologies, connected vehicles, drones, smart city technologies, and many others. These new log sources don't always send logs with Syslog and may utilize APIs, web services, or Cloud services specially built for logging. During planning for the collection of log data, and building a log collection platform, all of these new options must be considered.

> Welcome to brave new world of log collection using many methods to collect logs from Cloud, IoT, Vehicles, Drones, Operations Technologies, and others. Standing up a Syslog server is no longer sufficient but is still necessary as part of overall log collection strategy.

---

[1] Software as a Service

Focus of this chapter is to explore basic logging concepts, log sources, prioritization of logs, and building a simple and scalable log collection architecture.

3.1   Centralized or Distributed Log Collection?

A distributed log collection architecture where local log collectors receive logs from different log sources and then forward to one or more central locations is commonly used today. This architecture helps provide resiliency and reduction of loss of data in case communication link to central log collection becomes unavailable. Figure 3.1 shows one such arrangement.

A distributed architecture can collect as well as index log data locally at multiple locations and then make the indexes available to search requests. This may be necessary to meet certain regional privacy needs like GDPR[16] . However, one needs to balance the flexibility and scalability of distributed log collection infrastructure and the cost of managing it. As an example, indexing logs close to edge is attractive but it can create additional overhead in terms of correlation, reporting, alerting as well as cost of managing log indexes at multiple locations. Like everything else in life, there are some compromises to be made here as well!

3.2   Log Structure

Although structure of log messages from different log sources may vary slightly, there are some common fields that are usually part of every message. At minimum, log data will include:

- Logs are usually a time-series data and contain a time stamp that shows when message was created.

- Source IP address or host name to identify source of the log. The source does not need to be an IP address, though. For example, it may be a GUID (Globally Unique Identifier)[2] for some log sources, a VIN (Vehicle Identification Number) for a car, and so on.

- Message body which could be a text string, and in some cases, binary data that could be converted into a text string by the system analyzing the message. The body itself may be divided into many key-value pairs for additional fields.

There could be other fields in the log data as well. For example, message priority, the service or facility that created the message, message category and so on. Format of Syslog messages is defined in RFC5424 [19]. In some cases you may also prefer to use a gateway to convert different types of logs and then use Syslog as log transfer protocol for centralized logging. This is typically used to collect logs from Microsoft Windows systems.

> In some literature you may find term "event" which is usually a single log entry that contains interesting information. Sometimes another term "notable event" is also used that may refer to a subset of events that are more interesting for threat detection or other uses.

Product vendors usually provide information about structure of log messages created by their technologies. In other cases you may be able to configure a product to generate log messages based upon your preference or include/exclude specific key-value pairs in the log data.

---

[2]A GUID, sometimes also known as UUID or Universal Unique Identifier is a 128-bit number to uniquely identify an entity. If used properly, a GUID does not rely on any centralized registration authority and still provides unique identification

While typical log data is in simple text string format, logs may also be in many other formats including the following:

- CSV files

- XML documents

- JSON formatted logs

- Logs in binary formats

- Application logs with custom log format

You may have to use a log parser to convert logs from a specific format to one that SIEM can understand for analytics purpose.

3.3   Building a Scalable Log Collection Infrastructure

Building a log collection infrastructure that can scale as more log data is brought under SOC scope is crucial for long-term success of your project. A typical log collection architecture includes one or more local log collectors at each location. These collectors have local storage to temporarily store data in case communication links are not available. The log collectors should also be capable of collecting logs using multiple mechanisms including but not limited to Syslog, API calls, retrieving log files from individual systems and so on. Figure 3.1 shows a simplified diagram for a single site with one log collector forwarding logs to a central location.

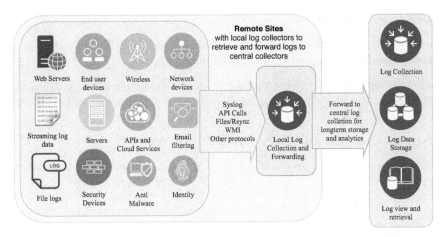

Figure 3.1: Building a scalable log collection infrastructure is crucial

Log collectors could be one or a combination of the following mechanisms. Specialized log collection mechanisms may be needed for modern log sources like connected vehicles, IoT systems, and others.

- A simple Linux machine running rSyslog [38] collector and forwarder

- Commercial log collectors that are included with different SIEM solutions

- A Windows machine that collects Windows logs and uses add-on software like Snare to forward these logs to a local or central collector

- A collector in Cloud environments such as AWS to collect logs using APIs and forward to central storage location

Syslog is a common and widely used protocol to collect logs over an IP network [19]. Typical log collection using Syslog infrastructure includes three roles as listed below [19].

- **Originator** is a system that is the source of log. It creates logs and sends it using Syslog protocol to a *Collector* or a *Relay*.

- **Collector** is a log receiver that collects logs either directly from the *Originator* or from *Relay*.

- **Relay** is an intermediate system that collects logs from *Originators* and relays these log messages to the *Collectors*. The *Relay* systems are used in large and distributed networks to collect logs at each locations and then send these logs to central log collectors.

The important aspect of log collection for a SOC project is that the methods and means should be standardized and documented for consistency purposes.

3.4   Selecting Log Sources

Some log sources are always important for threat detection and are listed below:

- Security logs including firewalls, IDS/IPS. proxy servers, email content filtering, VPN servers.

- Logs from authentication and authorization sources like directories, domain controllers and other authentication sources.

- Web server logs, especially logs from public web servers.

- Security services hosted in Cloud (such as Cloud based URL filtering solutions) and SaaS (Software-as-a-Service) applications hosted in the Cloud.

Based upon a phased approach to log management, the collection of log data from the above list is usually the first priority and is included in the initial phases of SOC deployment.

3.4.1   Approaches to Identify Valuable Logs

You can adopt one or more approaches to identify the best log sources for different phases of SOC implementation. These approaches may include threat modeling, asset classification, forensic significance and others.

3.4.2   Log Selection based upon Threat Modeling

As described in section 1.10, one potential approach to selecting logs is to perform threat modeling. In this approach, you consider potential adversaries, their methods of attacking your organization and how these attacks will manifest in log data. Based upon this analysis you can make a selection of the most valuable log sources. As the results of this exercise may be different for each organization, it is necessary that all organizations perform their own threat modeling.

Many organizations with mature Cybersecurity program have implemented controls to safeguard their digital assets. However, controls can give a false sense of security as many times mere existence of a control does not mean that it is (a) adequate and/or (b) effective. Protecting crown jewels requires continuous monitoring and evaluating controls. Following is a 5-step threat modeling process to improve resiliency of your program, identify and close gaps in log data collection. The process starts from identifying the digital assets you are most concerned about and potential attack scenarios and ends at building a business case to close any identified gaps.

Step 1 – What am I concerned about?

A typical starting point for threat modeling is to identify digital assets that you are more concerned about. A digital asset may be in different forms. It could be an overall system crucial for your business, a process, a data store where business critical data is stored, a specific piece of technology and so on. The important thing is that you select an asset based upon criticality to business operations. Some people may refer to the critical business assets as "crown jewels".

Step 2 – What could go wrong?

Once you have a digital asset identified, the next step is to brainstorm about:

- Who are potential threat actors (internal, external, partners, state sponsored, hectivists, financially motivated, corporate espionage, etc.)?

- Attack methods used by these threat actors (hacking, phishing, malware, physical, and others?

- How these attacks will manifest in detection mechanisms (logs, behavior/anamolies, network traffic etc.)?

Step 3 – What can protect from attack?

Here you are going to evaluate all controls in place to prevent and/or detect the attacks. These controls could be different flavors:

- Preventive controls that stop something bad from happening (firewalls, end point protection, IPS, etc.)

- Detective Controls like IDS, SIEM and others

- Administrative controls like policies, awareness programs

The important thing is to make sure that controls are (a) adequate and (b) effective. A firewall may be present but may not be properly configured. Similarly you may be using encryption but not managing keys properly. These are the examples where controls exist but not effective.

Step 4 – Is protection sufficient?

Based upon adequacy and evaluation of existing controls, you can estimate residual risk of a breach that may include a sum of multiple risk factors, including but not limited to:

- Business interruption risk

- Regulatory fines from different government agencies (e.g. Federal Trade Commission and SEC) or industry groups like PCI.

- Risk of data loss

- Impact to brand value

Step 5: How do I justify cost?

Creating a business case is one of the best ways to justify investment in Cybersecurity. Why you need funding? It may be for one of the following purposes:

- Add a new control because none exists

- Improve effectiveness of an existing control

- Replace an existing control with a better one

While there are many templates and recommendations about building business cases, one simple way is to focus on cost of doing it vs. cost of not doing it. There is a cost in both ways and if your cost of doing it is lower, only then it makes sense to request for funding.

Figure 3.2 shows this approach.

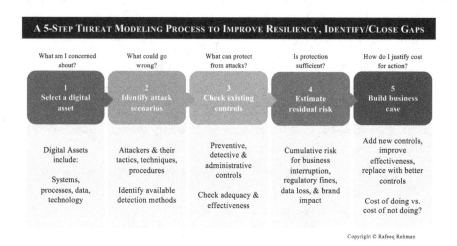

Figure 3.2: How to prioritize log sources based upon usefulness

3.4.3   Log Selection based upon Asset Classification

Another potential approach is to perform analysis on your most critical assets and identify log sources that will show an attack on these assets.

3.4.4   Log Selection based upon Forensic Importance

A third approach is thinking about utility of log in forensic investigations. In addition to logs that help identify malicious activity, some log sources may provide additional information and insights when you are investigating incidents. You may want to collect these logs as well and keep them for historical purposes. However, this should not be the first priority.

You can use Figure 3.3 as a sample table to score value of a log source to help prioritize it. Put an X in columns corresponding to each row if that column is relevant to that particular type of log source. In the right-most column, put a score by counting number of X in the row. The highest scoring log sources should be priority for initial phases of SOC implementation.

Figure 3.3 is an example of prioritization.

3.4.5   Using a phased approach

Whichever method you choose, you will always have more log data than you can effectively utilize. Make a selection for initial phase of your SOC implementation and then use a phased approach to bring more logs as your SOC become more mature and you are able to do something useful with the data you are collecting.

How to Prioritize Log Sources

Log Source	Usefulness for threat detection?	Required for compliance?	Related to business critical application?	Valuable for forensic investigation?	Total score
DMZ Firewall	X	X	X	X	4
URL Filtering Proxy	X	X		X	3
Ecommerce Apache Server	X	X	X	X	4
Development Web Server WAF				X	1

Figure 3.3: How to prioritize log sources based upon usefulness

3.4.6   What to do with logs?

Typically, you will build use cases in your Security Incident and Event Monitoring (SIEM) system and create alerts and incidents based upon these use cases. Although some logs may be collected only for forensic purposes, it would be wise to use maximum number of available log sources in creation of use cases.

3.4.7   Log retrieval and search

Most organizations keep only a small subset of data online and archive historical log data. An important aspect is that logs should be readily retrievable from any archive when you need them for investigations and be collected at a central location.

3.5   Security Log Sources

Technologies used to perform core information security tasks yield the best log data for threat detection and response. Collecting log data from these sources should be the first priority. Some of these technologies are listed below. While we do understand that every organization may not have all of these technologies implemented, you can easily start with these as your first phase of log collection.

- Network Intrusion Detection and Prevention Systems (IDS/IPS)
- Host based IDS
- Firewalls
- Proxy Servers
- VPN Concentrators
- Web App Firewalls
- Endpoint protection systems

- Data Loss Prevention (DLP) systems but be careful to handle sensitive data that may be in DLP logs
- Email/SPAM filtering
- Identify and Access management (IAM) Systems. Many organizations use Windows Active Directory domain controllers as part of identity management solution and these logs can be crucial. On the other hand, if you are using a Cloud based IAM system, make sure your Cloud identity provider is able to provide log collection option.
- Distributed Denial of Service (DDoS) technologies are mostly hosted by your Internet Service Provider (ISP) and could be useful in certain scenarios.
- Public Key Infrastructure (PKI) Systems
- Antivirus / Antimalware
- Cloud Access Security Broker (CASB)
- PKI (Public Key Infrastructure) systems

As many of these technologies are moving to Cloud, make sure logs are collected from Cloud service providers in addition to on-premises systems.

3.6　Server and System Logs

Server logs provide key insights for threat detection and response. First of all, make sure you start with collecting logs from servers used in the SOC itself. After that consider log collection from other servers based upon the criticality of applications running on these servers.

- Windows
- Linux
- UNIX/Other
- Mainframe etc.
- Virtualization technologies like OpenStack, VmWare, and others

3.7　Application Servers, Middleware and Business Systems

These are critical for business operations and provide a window into both employee and customer data. Attackers are mostly interested in getting access to these systems, enabling them find business data and exfilterate it. Following are some examples of servers or systems that you may be interested in getting logs from:

- Apache web server
- Other Web Servers and Application Servers
- Ecommerce Systems
- Databases
- Message Queues
- Order Management Systems

- HR Systems

- Configuration Management Systems

- Business Applications

- DevOps systems, deployment servers

In most scenarios, you don't have to collect logs from all of these systems in the initial phases of your SOC implementation. However, logs from Ecommerce web servers in a retail environment, for example, may be crucial for threat detection and response.

3.8 Netflow

Netflow is a UDP protocol designed for collecting data about network traffic. Typically, routers collect netflow data and forward it to a netflow collector system. This data can be used to identify network traffic anomalies, command and control (C&C) traffic, and other anomalies using machine learning algorithms. Netflow data provides excellent value for forensic investigations.

3.9 Applications

Log data from applications is challenging to handle for variety of reasons. Typically applications logs are either not readily available, or are not stored in an easy-to-use format. The logs that you do get usually don't follow standard conventions so you may have to write special log parsers. However, in some cases these logs could provide significant value or may be required to meet compliance needs. Consider the following categories when evaluating usefulness of application logs:

- Commercial Applications - You are limited by the log data generated by the application. You also have to work with the vendor to get information about the log format.

- Home grown applications - These are relatively easy as specific data can be logged by modifying the code. However, that will require additional expenses in development cost.

- Cloud applications - Most of the Cloud based applications do provide logging but retrieval of these logs may be a challenge.

Investigate log formats for each application and how to ingest data into SIEM technologies.

3.10 Cloud

Almost all businesses have a Cloud strategy as the push for moving applications to Cloud continues. Logs from Cloud environment are very crucial for threat detection and response capabilities as ultimately it is not the Cloud provider who is responsible for protecting your data in the Cloud but you! When considering Cloud data, think about the following:

- Log collection options provided by your Cloud vendor. Some Cloud vendors may provide raw log data using shared storage while others may provide APIs to enable you collect logs. It is crucial to understand all available options and which of the options will work best for you. The best approach may be a combination of multiple options depending upon how many Cloud vendors you use.

- The type of Cloud service also matters. Log collection for Infrastructure as a Service (IaaS) vendor may be different than a vendor who is providing you Software as a Service

(SaaS) Cloud. For IaaS Cloud, you can typically collect logs for all layers of the IT stack whereas in the case of SaaS, you may get only application logs.

- In many IaaS services, you can host virtual security devices (VPN, FIrewalls, etc.) inside the Cloud. Collecting logs from these devices is as crucial as collecting logs from other security devices inside your corporate network or corporate data centers.

Many organizations have started implementing Cloud Access Security Broker (CASB) solutions to add an extra layer of security between corporate data centers and Cloud service providers. CASB logs should also be considered in the initial phases of SOC implementation.

3.11   Internet of Things (IoT)

Some industries are implementing IoT technologies more rapidly compared to others. IoT security is a topic in itself as these technologies bring new aspects that are not part of traditional network and IT security. These aspects include, but not limited to, different network protocols for IoT devices, security of firmware updates/consistency, non-interactive authentication and authorization, and so on. If IoT is a crucial part of your business, you should prioritize collecting and processing IoT logs appropriately.

3.12   Mobile and Handheld Devices

If your business manage mobile and handheld devices, you may be using a Mobile Device Management (MDM) system. Typically forwarding logs from MDM to centralized log collection systems is the first good step for managing mobile device security.

3.13   Operational Technologies (OT) SCADA/ICS

Operational Technologies (OT) are mostly relevant in industrial environment, oil and gas sector, power generation and transmission. This requires a different skill set and in many cases OT SOC is managed separately. However, with IT and OT convergence in many industries, a modern SOC is really a converged SOC that handles both IT and OT environment. OT logs are coming from Programmable Logic Controllers (PLCs), Industrial Control Systems (ICS), Supervisory Control And Data Acquisition (SCADA) systems etc.

When dealing with OT logs and OT related incidents, make sure that SOC personnel are trained on OT systems as security considerations for OT are not exactly the same as general IT systems. Availability and safety are more important in OT world compared to confidentiality in the case of IT systems.

> Data from sensitive networks can be collected using technologies that allow one-way data transfer at the hardware level such that there is no way to reach back to the sensitive network. In general, these technologies are called "data diode". If you want to enable data collection from the OT network but also want to make sure there is no reverse path, please consider use of data diode hardware.

3.14   Physical Security Logs

Depending upon needs of your organization, physical security may be crucial and log data from physical security systems may be valuable for SOC. If the SOC scope includes physical security, identify all logs sources from physical security systems and prioritize them based upon their overall value. You may have to write special use cases and alerts for physical systems security and a different type of incident response plan.

3.15 Full Network Packet Capture Data

While not typically done in the initial phase of a SOC, full packet capture data is valuable in many scenarios but it could be expensive. Newer and Cloud-based solutions can provide needed functionality, scalability, and cost management. Packet data is also very useful in incident investigation.

3.16 Logging and NAT

In many networks, Network Address Translation (NAT) is commonly used for different reasons. NAT enables altering source or destination IP addresses during data packet's journey through the network. However, this may create serious issues for log collection infrastructure and to identify the true source of log data. If log sources in your network are behind a NAT router, make sure you find means to overcome his issue. Different log collectors, relays, and forwarders have the capability to overcome the NAT issues. RFC 1918 [21].

Another typical problem in NATed networks is overlapping IP addresses in different segments of a network. An analysis of network to identify this issue in initial phases can save trouble later on.

3.17 Logging and Network Time Protocol

A timestamp is an essential part of each log event. An important factor in building logging infrastructure is to ensure time synchronizing among all log sources to keep proper order of logs, necessary for correlation. Network Time Protocol (NTP) is commonly used for purpose. While NTP is a topic in itself, it is sufficient at this point to understand that no logging infrastructure is complete until NTP is implemented to support it. Without it, log correlation and analytics will not work properly as logs are a time-series data.

Timestamp is a necessary part of log data to understand what happened and when it happened. Network Time Protocol (NTP) [35] [11] is a key protocol to keep time on all log sources synchronized. This is crucial to ensure that all logs can be placed in a chronological order when collected from a number of different sources.

NTP is a client-server protocol where the server is a standard time source and clients synchronize their local clock with the server on continuous basis. Many standard NTP servers are available on the Internet [34] and you can setup an internal NTP server that takes its time from the standard time sources.

3.18 Logging Policy and Standards

Lastly, building logging standards to identify type, amount, and level of logging also goes a long way to build a consistent approach throughout an organization. A logging standard must address requirements for logging at different levels including system, middleware, and applications. The logging standards should also specify accepted logging protocols, storage and lifecycle of log data. Logging policy and standards must be updated at least on annual basis to ensure new sources and types of important logs are taken into consideration based upon their value.

Processes and standards for log collection play a crucial role for adding new log sources. There should be defined roles and responsibilities about who manages log sources and ensures logs are being forwarded, the types of logs that should be forwarded, log collection agents needed for collecting log data, and so on. These policies and standards should be part and parcel of overall SOC operational processes.

3.19 Sample Log Prioritization

A common question is where to start collecting logs and other telemetry data? Table 3.1 shows a sample list of prioritized log sources that will help you make some decisions based upon where you are on your journey to build SOC. The list of log sources shown under foundational log data is the best starting point. Once you have covered the basic logs, then you can move to more advanced sources and/or specialty log data based upon your requirements.

Have "more data" is not necessarily a good thing always. The more logs you collect, the more storage and processing capacity you need. My recommendation is that you should assess the needs and have a plan to productively use these data sources instead of just a big dump of log data.

3.20 Chapter Summary and Recommendations

- A scalable log collection architecture and logging standards are necessary and foundational to build a successful SOC.

- You need to work with extended IT, network, and application owners to forward logs from a diverse set of systems. You also need their help to deploy and manage logging infrastructure (forwarder, relays, collectors).

- There are always more logs than you can collect and use in productive manner. This necessitates prioritization of logs based upon their usefulness for security monitoring and alerting. Use a phased approach to collect the most important logs first.

- You should always be mindful about the cost of log collection, storage, and processing. Many SIEM vendors license their products based upon the log volume and *collecting all logs* may become cost-prohibitive very quickly.

- Many time, compliance needs mandate collection, storage and processing of specific types of logs from specific systems.

- Use of local log collectors that could help in reliability, buffering, compression and bandwidth saving.

- Use of NTP is crucial for getting correct log time stamps and proper correlation.

- Understanding that modern log collection needs support of diverse log collection mechanisms that include Syslog, APIs, IoT protocols like MQTT[36], plain text files, XML, binary logs and others.

- Build policies and logging standards to bring consistency and clarity of logging requirements.

- A mechanism to detect missing logs must be part of log collection.

Log Type	List of log sources
Foundational log sources	These are the log sources that you should absolutely start with as minimum: 1. Firewall 2. IDS/IPS 3. Windows, Linux and other servers 4. DNS 5. VPN and remote access systems 6. Web proxy, Cloud based proxy solutions 7. Web Application Firewalls (WAF) 8. Endpoint Detection and Response (EDR) systems 9. Network devices (routers, switches, wireless access points) 10. Email 11. Identity and Access Management 12. Host based IDS/IPS 13. File Integrity Monitoring (FIM) - This is usually also needed for compliance
Advanced level log sources	Once you have the initial set of log sources, consider adding the following to your list for additional context and enrich correlation. 1. Cloud logs collected through APIs 2. Apache and other web/application server logs 3. Middleware, message queues, business applications, ERP systems 4. DLP 5. DDoS protection systems 6. PKI 7. Cloud Access Security Broker (CASB) 8. Network telemetry data in the form of NetFlows 9. Full packet or pcap data
Specialty log sources	These are more advanced and specialty log sources that everyone may not need. 1. IoT 2. Operational Technologies (OT, SCADA, ICS) 3. Specialty logs based upon certain emerging technologies like drones, connected cars etc. 4. Physical security systems

Table 3.1: Sample table for log source prioritization

— I choose a lazy person to do a hard job because a lazy person will find an easy way to do it.

Bill Gates

— Hire character, train skills

Peter Schutz

4

SOC Human Resources

Motivated, experienced and knowledgeable SOC engineers are key to success of any SOC. Continuous improvement, automation, and finding simpler methods to detect threats are essential and that is why you need innovative and motivated people who take initiatives to explore new ideas. The field of information security is changing fast and a continuous learning and relearning is key to success for people working in a SOC. Only motivated people who are enthusiastic about information security will succeed in this environment. This chapter is to explore roles and responsibilities of SOC team.

There are some common personality characteristics for SOC analysts that could make one a good fit for the job. These personality traits include, but are not limited to, the following:

- Curiosity to know more

- An attitude of continuous learning

- Ability to work under pressure

- Stay calm, and be patient

- An understanding of risk and making timely judgment calls

While the skills are important to work in SOC, the personality traits are even more crucial as SOC professionals deal with uncertainties and new threats on daily basis. SOC analysts will always be open to new ideas and question old assertions to accurately detect, analyze and mitigate threats.

One common question is how many people are needed to run an effective SOC? The number and type of people needed to run a SOC depends upon SOC operations model and scope of responsibilities owned by SOC team. Defining human resource needs is one of the key element of SOC planning because it is part of building business case and budget needs. Later in this chapter you will see answers to this question.

4.1   SOC Operation Time

The SOC operations times could have multiple options. For example:

- A 24x7x365 operations means that SOC is open 24 hours a day, 365 days a year.

- A 8x5x5 operations SOC is open during business hours from 8 AM to 5 PM in working days only.

- Some businesses will run internal SOC for one or two shifts during the day and outsource the rest of it to a managed security services provider.

- Some organizations may choose to have two shifts in working days and have someone on-call for the third shift.

Assuming that your are building a single-location SOC, the time of operation is the first parameter that will go into calculating number of people needed in the SOC team.

Scope of SOC Responsibilities

While there are essential elements of a SOC including analysts and incident responders, there are many other areas that may or may not be part of SOC activities. For example, a vulnerability management program may be run under a separate team or could be part of SOC organizations. Similarly, some functions, like forensic investigation, may be outsourced to third parties.

Based upon the decisions made about scope of SOC responsibilities, number of people needed to run an effective SOC may be quite different. This chapter is about exploring roles and responsibilities for different situations and the skill set needed for these roles.

4.2   How many People do I Need?

The estimate for number of people may vary significantly different depending upon whether you want to run a 24x7x365 SOC or something less than that. Following is one way of estimating number of people for 24x7x365 SOC.

Consider three shifts of 8 hours each. Also, consider 3 analysts in first shift and 2 analysts for each of the other two shifts. This will make 7 analysts on daily basis with 8 hours work time each, resulting in a total 56 hours every day. For the whole year (365 days), this will require 20,440 hours. Let us make it an even number of 20,000 for the sake of simplicity. Typically, one person will work for 2000 hours on annual basis when we account for vacation and holidays. This means you need 10 analysts to run the SOC. You can divide these analysts into tier 1, tier 2 and tier 3. In this example, I estimate 5 tier 1 analysts, 3 tier 2 analysts and 2 tier 3 analysts.

In addition to analysts, you will also need specialists like forensics and malware experts, manage SIEM platform, build new use cases, and one or more SOC managers and team leads.

If the SOC operations is not 24x7x365, your estimates will change accordingly. Based upon number of shifts, you have to create a schedule for these analysts and plan for vacation, training, and other situations. Typically, a SOC manager will be responsible for managing the team, scheduling, training, hiring and establishing relationships across the organization.

Following is a typical SOC team for a 24x7x365 operations. It is based upon assumption of a medium size organization and single SOC. For large organization and multiple/distributed SOC, the team could be quite large.

1. SOC manager - minimum one (1)

2. Tier 1 to tier 3 analysts - minimum ten (10)

3. SOC infrastructure architect/engineer - minimum one (1) but preferably two (2)

4. Forensic analyst - minimum one (1) or outsourced to an outside vendor

5. SIEM content/use case developer - minimum one (1)

6. CIRT/CSIRT - minimum one (1), multiple people needed for a 24x7 operations

7. Vulnerability management - minimum one (1)

As you can see from the list above, you would need 15-16 people to run a SOC even after combining few roles. The number goes up quite significantly for larger organizations. An important part of SOC planning is to effectively define these roles and responsibilities for managing cost and risk. Over last 15 years, I have seen many SOC implementations, interviewed many SOC managers and CISOs, and have developed some models for organizations of varying needs. It is really a combination of science and art to build a SOC team.

> **PITFALL: Building SOC with too few people**
>
> When you are constrained by budget, it is tempting to build a SOC with too few people, stretching them work longer hours and on weekends or on call on week days. If you take that route, you will end up a very unsatisfied SOC staff with low retention rate resulting in ultimate failure to achieve your objectives.

4.3 SOC Organizational Chart, Job Roles and Skills Definitions

A typical SOC organization can be described with a chart such as shown in Figure 4.1. Some roles shown in this chart may be combined under one person, some may be a team in itself, and some may be outsourced to service providers. For example, you may not need a full time forensic investigator and may decide to utilize an external vendor on as-needed basis for this purpose.

Following is a brief description of these roles:

- **SOC Manager** has the overall responsibility for managing the operations, scheduling staff for SOC shifts, training the staff, and SOC processes.

- **SIEM Architect or Engineer** provides expertise in designing, implementation, and operations of SIEM solution (or any other technology for collecting, analyzing, and managing logs). This person may also be tasked with creating and tuning use cases and alerts. Depending upon size of the SOC, this role is divided into two sub-roles in many cases:

  - A SIEM infrastructure architect/engineer who is responsible for managing the SIEM infrastructure, log collection, fine tuning of the SIEM technologies, patching and upgrades.

  - A SIEM content developer responsible for building and fine tuning use cases, integrating threat intelligence, automation, and continuous improvement in threat detection.

- **SOC Analysts** are responsible for day to day operations, analyzing alerts, assigning priorities, and taking remediation actions.

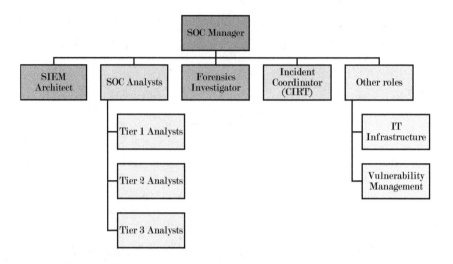

Figure 4.1: SOC Organization Chart

- **Forensic Investigator** has deep expertise in doing forensic analysis to find root cause of incidents, threat actors, and use threat intelligence sources to get to the bottom of an incident. In some cases, tier 3 analysts also have expertise in forensic investigations.

- **Incident Coordinator** also known as CIRT (Cyber/Computer Incident Response Team) is responsible to manage lifecycle for security incidents from start to end. Typically the SOC Analysts will create incidents after their analysis and the CIRT will take the ownership to remediate and close an incident. Incident responders work broader IT teams, identify players who will carry out remediations tasks, and take the ownership of incidents until closure. Sometimes this ream is also referred as CSIRT (Computer Security Incident Response Team).

- **IT Infrastructure** teams provide support for managing SOC technology infrastructure (network, servers, storage, and others).

- **Vulnerability Management** person will be responsible for network and application vulnerability scanning and utilize the results of scanning for integrating into SIEM. Depending upon size of the organization, you may need a team of people for vulnerability management program.

When planning for SOC, build the organization chart even if you don't plan to fill all positions in a SOC organization. A more expanded description of these roles is in the next section.

Why CISO is not part of organization chart

Note that a CISO is not included in the organizational chart as a typical CISO role will focus on oversight rather than day-to-day operations of SOC.

4.4 Job Roles and Skills Definitions

Hiring right people is a crucial human resources (HR) function. Typically HR advertises job openings with a job description and job responsibilities. Although the actual job description could be quite detailed, following are some key responsibilities of each of the job functions. As mentioned earlier, while hiring SOC personnel, attitude and personality is as important as skills.

4.4.1 CISO

Typical CISO role is not responsible for day-to-day SOC operations but has important responsibilities for governance.

- Develop and implement a security program, including cross-functional SOC governance board.
- Provide overall vision and direction for SOC, incident response and risk management.
- Hire, retain, and train security staff to meet objectives of security program.
- Keep the risk at a manageable level.
- Communicate security risk to non-security management, partner with business leaders.
- Understand threat landscape and lead teams to take counter measure when necessary.

4.4.2 SOC Manager

SOC managers run the show. There may be more than one SOC managers, or a combination of SOC manager and team leads.

- Build partnerships with other IT teams and SOC governance board.
- Define and implement SOC policies and procedures.
- Define metrics, report SOC performance and improvements to leadership.
- Hire and train employees.
- Manage SOC budget.
- Manage SOC shifts in case of a 24x7x365 operations.
- Plan for SOC expansion and continuous improvements.
- Maintain a risk register .
- Work with service providers in case some SOC functions are outsourced.
- Plan for and execute technology upgrades and security patches.
- Maintain relationships with industry organizations, ISACs (Information Sharing and Analysis Center), law enforcement and others.

4.4.3 SIEM Architect, Engineer, and SIEM Content Developer

Depending upon SOC size, this could be split into multiple roles. The basic idea is to ensure that technologies used to operate SOC are properly design, implemented and kept up to date. The technology stack is complicated and needs continuous care/updates to keep it effective and relevant.

- Architect, design and implement SOC technology stack.

- Provide technology roadmap.

- Capacity planning for SOC technology.

- Business continuity and disaster recovery planning, testing the plans.

- Apply security patches and updates.

- Threat modeling to identify vulnerabilities, threat actors, counter measures and build methods to identify and alert on activities of threat actors.

- Create new SIEM use cases based upon threat models and test efficiency of existing use cases.

- Automate routine tasks either through scripting or using technologies like SOAR (Security Orchestration, Automation and Response).

- Integrate threat intelligence.

4.4.4   Security Analysts - Tier 1 to tier 3

A typical SOC will have three tiers of SOC analysts for optimal operations.

- *Tier 1* analysts are the first point of contact for alerts generated through SIEM and other technologies, receive calls from other departments, perform basic analysis, remove false positives, respond to known issues. They act as the front line of SOC operations.

- *Tier 2* analysts work on issues escalated by tier 1 analysts, provide guidance to tier 1 analysts. For any new type of incidents, they will recommend solutions and instructions to implement these solutions. They will also update SOC knowledge base articles for future reference of Tier 1 employees.

- *Tier 3* analysts are seasoned SOC professionals who work on improving efficiency of SOC, automate tasks, provide forensic support, look for patterns to help prevent future incidents. Tier 3 is also responsible for consulting roles for other IT teams. They may be involved in other proactive activities such as threat hunting.

4.4.5   Incident Response Coordinator

This is a CIRT/CSIRT role. For small to medium size SOC, few people in the role would be enough. However, for larger SOC and depending upon number of incidents, you may have to build a team for ensuring proper and timely closure of security incidents.

- Maintain an incident response plans and partnership with other teams.

- Coordinate mitigation activities across the IT organizations.

- Prioritize activities.

- Manage incident lifecycle such that when an incident is created by the analysts, it is taken to closure.

- Report on incidents workload for security leadership.

- Conducting *Lessons Learned* exercises to improve overall security and efficiency of IT operations.

- Identify trends to understand systematic problems and solve these problems through problem management processes.

4.4.6 Forensic Investigator

Forensic investigators will work CSIRT team for deeper level of investigations into security incidents, find root cause, analyze malware and other related activities.

- Use tools to collect, analyze and preserve data.

- Create forensic images of running systems. Understand different operating systems thoroughly.

- Sometimes a forensic investigator may have to work with mobile devices, phones, IoT and other specialized hardware.

- Identify compromised systems and evaluate timeline for the compromise.

- Create processes for investigations.

- Be familiar with contemporary systems and applications and related vulnerabilities.

- Understand applicable laws and protect evidence.

- Be part of incident response processes and procedures.

Forensic investigators also need to have great communications skills as they will be writing forensic reports and may be called in as expert witness in courts of law.

4.4.7 Other roles

In addition to the above mentioned roles, you may have the following job functions assigned to employees as their secondary roles.

- Malware analysis

- Network and application vulnerability management.

- Threat intelligence feed evaluations.

- Managing underlying IT infrastructure.

- Chief supply chain manager to keep Mountain Dew rack filled all the time :)

4.4.8 Combining SOC Roles

For smaller organizations, some of the roles in SOC organizational chart could be combined under a single person. For example, forensic investigator could also perform vulnerability scanning responsibilities. Similarly, you may decide to combine level 2 and level 3 analyst roles.

4.5 Finding and Recruiting SOC Analysts

Finding and retaining qualified SOC personal is a challenge due to shortage of available talent. The SOC analyst is also a challenging and stressful job. For these reasons, building a cohesive team is utmost important to keep the staff engaged. Finding people through referrals usually works better.

Another approach is to hire a mix of senior and junior analysts and create a clear career path for junior analysts.

The last recommendation is that hire for *attitude to learn* compared to focusing on existing skills. The reason is that security field is changing fast and any existing skills will be obsolete soon. So any person will be a good fit if he/she has good and positive attitude towards continuously learn, unlearning, and relearning.

4.6   Training and Certifications

Continuous learning and updating skills is key to success of any security program. The SOC manager must create a program and career path for SOC staff such that they can continuously learn and advance their skills.

There are many training and certification opportunities as listed below:

Common certifications for SOC teams include:

- **Certified Information Systems Security Professional (CISSP)** is considered a great certification for all security professionals.

- **Certified Ethical Hacker (CEH)** can be a good certification at a starting level.

- **Security+** certification from CompTIA is great entry level certification for security analysts as well as for vulnerability scanners.

- **EC-Council Certified Security Analyst (ECSA)** is a great certification for security analysts.

- **Vendor-Specific Certifications** are also available from security vendors and are helpful if you are using commercial software and tools.

- **SANS certifications** are excellent for acquiring skills for forensic investigations [24].

For SOC managers, it is better to make sure each SOC staff member has a *Personal Development* goal and attaining new certification is part of that goal.

4.6.1   Training on Free Sources

There are many free training and learning opportunities available. Some of these are as listed here but you can find areas of your interest and make it part of personal development goals.

- Verizon Data Breach Investigations Report (DBIR) and other reports so that SOC analysts understand attack patterns and keep themselves up-to-date on emerging threats

- ENISA provide free training courses online [15].

- Training material is available from Cloud Security Alliance.

- Coursera [9] has many security courses free for students who don't need to earn a certificate. Other sites like EDX [13] and Udacity [41] also provide a wide selection of security courses.

Security vendors have free webinars that could be useful for the SOC staff. Many recorded webinars are available at BrightTalk [6].

4.6.2 SOC Knowledge base as a Training Tool

An internal knowledge base system is essential for SOC. It could be as simple as a WiKi limited to SOC staff so that they can add knowledge base entries as they discover new things. It can be used as a training tool for new hires.

4.6.3 Other Training Options

- Vendors training programs

- Books - It is a good idea to continuously purchase new and updated books for SOC

- Conferences

- Encouraging SOC staff to write white papers. Writing in itself is a great training exercise as it forces one to do research on the topic of writing.

4.7 Career progression paths

As mentioned earlier, it is crucial for SOC staff to have a growth and career development plan to keep them engaged. Good managers are always focused on how they can help their team members move to the next level in their career.

4.8 Writing Job Descriptions

At some point you are going to write and post job description to hire SOC staff. Your human resources departments probably has some standards and formats for job posting. My recommendation is to have each job post divided into the following sections.

1. **Where will you work?** - Describe your organization that would attract talented people. This is your opportunity to market your organization and why someone should be interested in working with you.

2. **What will you do?** - Explain the type of work an employee will be doing. Don't take standard corporate job description, write your own.

3. **What skills are required?** - List essential skills required for this job but don't go overboard. There is no need to write the standard "three to five years experience" with every skill. Remember you want to hire for attitude, skills can be acquired. Keep in mind that any past skills will become outdated soon. People with right attitude will continuously learn new skills and update existing ones.

Building the right team of professionals is key. Most of the people will get the right technology but building a great team is hard. If you are a SOC manager or CISO, your primary job is to develop and serve your team. If you are able to do so everything else will fall into its place.

4.9 Chapter Summary and Recommendations

- A SOC organization chart is a good starting point for staff planning, even when you don't plan to fill all roles. An organization chart is also essential for SOC budget calculation.

- Roles are responsibilities for each person in SOC should be well-defined.

- Referrals are a great way to find good candidates for SOC and build a well-connected team.

- Managers should work on making training and certification part of personal development plan.

- Create an internal Wiki for knowledge base.

- SOC analyst is a stressful job. Managers should make all efforts to make it as easy as possible.

- Each person working in SOC must have a career development plan.

Part II

Building SOC

Just because something doesn't do what you planned it to do doesn't mean it's useless.

Thomas Edison

More technology and tools are not always a good thing. If you don't have people to effectively use tools, it may become a liability.

Anonymous

5

SOC Technology Stack

The focus of this chapter is on finding the right technology stack for a Security Operations Center. However, I would like to start with two fictional stories.

Realizing a changing threat landscape, the board of directors put their support behind efforts for better protection of their customers' data and the brand. The company hired a new CISO and doubled the budget for information risk management. The CISO was thrilled! She put an ambitious plan together including building a security operations center. The best SIEM technology was purchased. The SIEM vendor installed and turned ON default alerts. Everyone celebrated success sharing of screenshots of fancy dashboards and colorful graphs. However that was just the beginning. The real story started from that point onwards!

After the SIEM vendor left, the staff started realizing that the number of alerts they receive are overwhelming. Most of the time was wasted in pursuing alerts that were false positives triggered by default use cases. They badly needed an expert person on staff to fine tune and calibrate the alerts to separate noise from interesting data. However, the CISO had spent most of additional budget in purchasing the SIEM. There was not much left to bring any external consultants, or hire permanent employees for fine tuning.

Here is the story of another organization. The CISO, who knew a very talented, technical, hands-on friend for a number of years. Let us call him the *"wizard"*. As soon as the CISO got a new position approved, she hired the "wizard" immediately. The *wizard* considered commercial tools lacking in features here and there. He customized everything, wrote complex scripts, used many open sources tools and made things work. Until the day he got another offer from a different company that he could not refuse and resigned. Things worked for few months, until new patches started coming in with incompatibilities to libraries used in the scripts that *the wizard* had built. There was no one else on the team who understood the complexities in what the *wizard* had built and everything started falling apart. The CISO found herself looking for standards based approaches and dismantling the *wizardry* as it could not be supported in the long run.

5.1   Typical Root Causes of SOC Failures

Although the above stories are fictional they are very close to reality. I have seen this play out in different forms and fashions throughout my career. While researching for this book, I interacted with many security practitioners in past few years and heard many other SOC failure as well as success stories. Although characters and circumstances change but the *root causes* for most of the SOC failures stays the same:

- Failure to understand the bigger picture of *"total cost of ownership"* of a SOC.

- Getting carried away by a notion of buying *"the best tools available"* and not realizing that no tool work without competent SOC staff and continuous fine tuning, no matter how sophisticated or expensive they are.

- Relying too much on certain individuals instead of standards often results in trouble when these individuals leave, which they always do for better career options.

- Lack of managing expectations of stakeholders or understanding of specifics of a company culture.

Keeping these in mind, one needs to carefully research and plan not only for purchasing technology stack but also for its maintenance and effectiveness in threat management. More technology is not necessarily always a good thing. Depending upon the size and scope of a SOC, technology could still be a significant portion of capital budget. While some technology components are basic *requirements* for SOC, others may be *nice to have*.

5.2   Essential SOC Technology Stack

The foundational and required technologies for a SOC include:

- Log collection infrastructure that enables reliable transfer of logs from the log source to a central log collection and storage facility. As some of you may have observed, many vendors are also enabling threat detection on the "edge" and sending alerts to SOC team instead just sending raw logs. Endpoint Detection and Response (EDR) tools are a prime example of such technologies. However, even for the technologies that are able to detect threats on the edge, raw log storage is still needed for compliance and, sometimes, for investigation purposes.

- A Security Incident and Event Management (SIEM) system that processes log data, performs correlations and generates incidents and alerts.

- An asset database and vulnerability scanning/assessment tool that shows business criticality of different assets and vulnerabilities to help determine urgency of remediation tasks.

- Incident lifecycle management including ticketing system and workflow tools.

In addition to the above, there are a number of supporting technologies and tools that you would like to have for accommodating other aspects of daily operations. These include:

- Excellent reporting tools for generating dashboards and reports. Many times, some reporting options are available within SIEM tools. In other cases you will use separate technologies to build reports and dashboards.

- Forensic tools and forensic labs to properly protect and store evidence.

- Network and application vulnerability scanning tools to maintain up-to-date vulnerability database associated with assets.

- Threat intelligence gathering and integration into and automation with SIEM and other security devices such as firewalls, web content filtering etc.

- Tools for collecting data other than traditional logs (e.g. NetFlow data, full packet capture data, collecting data from Cloud services through APIs, and so on). With more and more communications being encrypted, full packet capture is losing some of its value unless there is an "encryption free" zone to inspect network data.

- Something like internal WiKi for knowledge management.

Every tool does not need to be commercial. Open source tools will suffice for a number of needs listed above.

As shown in Figure 5.1, the SOC technology stack functions can be divided into four layers. These layers are summarized as:

1. The *"Get Data"* layer includes technologies used to collect and transfer logs to a central location

2. The *"Add Context"* layer provides functions to add context to the log data. Vulnerability scanning tools not only identify what needs to be done but also add context to the log data and help determine severity of an event.

3. The *"Alert/SIEM"* technologies implement use cases to correlate the data and generate alerts

4. Technologies at the *"Respond"* layer are used to respond to incidents and perform remediation tasks

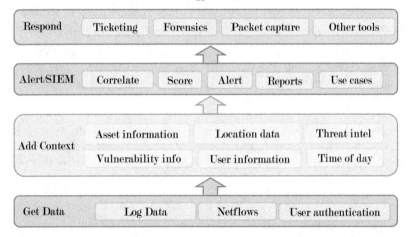

Figure 5.1: SOC Technology Stack Functions

The intention of the following sections is to explore options for building a technology stack. Once again, you should think about a phased approach for building the technology stack starting with essential components.

5.3   SIEM

Security Information and Event Management (SIEM) system is at the core of a SOC. It may not be a single product and could be a combination of many tools. Most commercial SIEM solutions are capable of performing a number of tasks including but not limited to the following:

- Log collection, storage and analysis.

- Event correlations by taking into account multiple log sources, vulnerability data, and other sources of information[1].

- Dashboards and reports.

- Managing account and role based access to the SIEM solution.

- Alerting capability using multiple mechanisms.

- Retaining logs for a certain period of time for compliance purposes.

- Provide log search capability to help in investigations of security incidents.

In addition to commercial SIEM solutions, a number of open source software packages are also available. While selecting a SIEM solution, you may want to consider the following:

- Cost is always a major factor. Consumption based licensing can add to overall cost. You should compare different consumption based cost models including CPU socket vs data ingestion volume.

- Types of logs that the solution is capable of ingesting without writing log parsers

- Maturity of the solution

- Whether the solution is available for on premises implementation, in the Cloud, or both

- Scalability

- Support of distributed architecture to comply with requirements of storing data in different regions (e.g. compliance to General Data Protection Regulation - GDPR[16])

In case of the open source solutions, you should also consider the type of open source license and support options available for the solution. You should also look into long term viability of the open source software, the size of the community who has adopted the solution and how active the project is when it comes to new features development.

> One of the major issues I have seen over and over is the lack of ability to properly ingest variety of log data. This usually happens when you have already implemented SIEM with initial set of logs and start adding more log sources. At that time you start realizing that your solution can't properly understand the additional log types. Writing log parsers becomes a significant operational overhead.

Log collecting and forwarding to SIEM usually needs additional engineering and should not be an afterthought. Some SIEM solutions come with their own methods for log forwarding whereas other SIEM solutions may require add-on components. Building a scalable log collection infrastructure is crucial for successful implementation of SIEM. Please refer to section 3.3 of this book for further information on how to build log collection infrastructure and how to collect telemetry data beyond syslog messages.

---

[1]Slow-moving attacks may be able to evade event correlation and threat hunting is necessary to detect these attacks

---

Do all SIEM solutions provide realtime threat detection?

An important consideration is how the SIEM technology *implements* correlations and threat detection activities. Some SIEM solutions use timed searches for threat detection that are not realtime. Others rely on data streams such that threat detection happen while the log data is being processed to provide a more realtime detection of threats. While evaluating SIEM technologies, you must go beyond marketing brochures and glossy slides and dig deeper into how the technology works under the hood.

5.4 Use Case Development

The SIEM solutions implementation is not a one-time job. Continuous updates will be required as new threats are discovered and new log sources are integrated to the overall solution. New use cases need to be built and existing ones need to be fine tuned based upon scenarios that you are concerned about. A SIEM engineer/architect or a SIEM content developer role is necessary for the SOC team to continuously work on use case development.

A scenario for building use cases is typically something that you are concerned about and need to be alerted when it happens. For example, you may be concerned about ransomware propagation inside your network and want to build a use case to detect when it happens.

While many commercial SIEM solutions come bundled with use cases that you can enable/disable, default use cases may create significant noise and overwhelm the SOC team investigating events that don't matter much. A better option could be disabling every default use case and enable them one by one after performing threat analysis and some fine tuning. Many times SOC teams build their own custom use cases based upon specific needs and to address scenarios that are more important for them. Figure 5.2 shows steps that you should take while building custom use cases, or even fine tuning existing use cases. My advice is to start with threat modeling, build a scenario, understanding the threat actors, the actions they will take and how these actions will manifest in logs. Please refer to sections 1.10 and 3.4.2 for more information about threat modeling.

As shown in Figure 5.2, a disciplined and systematic approach is necessary to obtain optimal results. Following this step-by-step model brings consistency and improves quality of detection and response. A process flow accompanied with a checklist for use case development is very helpful.

Documenting guidelines and actions for each use case

What happens when a use case is triggered and it creates an alert? Documenting guidelines or checklists for responding to these alerts is an essential part of the use case development process. Every SOC analyst may not have necessary background and knowledge that went into development of the use case. It will be very helpful to have access to guidelines and required actions for responding to alerts triggered by each use case.

5.4.1 Planning Use Case Roll Out

Testing, fine tuning, and using a change control process to roll out any new use cases is crucial for SOC success. Testing must include that a use case does not miss real events and does not create false positives resulting wasted time in investigations.

ACTOR - Define the threat actor you want to protect against. This will help understand tactics, techniques, and procedures used by the threat actors

 ACTION - Identify actions taken by the threat actor. These actions may already be logged. If not, make sure enable logging for these actions.

 LOG SOURCES - Which log sources will have information about the actions? There could be more than one log sources where actions are logged.

 INDICATORS - Within the log sources, find indicators of actions taken by the threat actors? These indicators may be keywords, specific events, etc.

 BUILD USE CASE - Based upon indicators, build use cases to detect and alert on the activity of the threat actor. Exclude legitimate activity from alerts.

 TEST & APPROVE - Test the use cases with sample data, false positive positives and false negatives. Get approvals from stakeholders.

 ROLL OUT TO PRODUCTION - Use change control process to roll out the new use cases to production environment

Figure 5.2: Use Case development process

Before rolling out a new or updated use case, SOC staff must be trained on:

- The scenario description and what this use case means
- The logs sources that trigger the use cases alerts
- The actions that the SOC staff needs to take when they see this use case triggered

5.4.2   Use Case Performance

Monitoring performance of new uses cases over a period of time should also be part of the plan. This is necessary to identify *effectiveness* as well as need for fine tuning.

Another important aspect of use case performance is the *impact* of SIEM rules on CPU/memory utilization. Some SIEM rules may adversely impact SIEM with very expensive queries in terms of time and resources needed to run these queries. Testing CPU/memory impact of a use case must be part of use case testing and roll out process.

5.4.3   Use Case Log Book

Over time, you will build new use cases, fine tune existing use cases, or incorporate new use cases provided by external vendors (or your SIEM provider). Maintaining a history of these use cases in a log book is an essential part of SOC management. Table 5.1 provides a sample log book for keeping track of use cases.

Use case ID	Use case name	Description and solution	Log/data sources	SIEM rules and alerts	Remediation guideline
1	*A short name for the use case*	*Describe the problem use case solves*	*List data sources needed to implement this use case*	*List SIEM rules and alerts that implement this use case*	*A brief guideline for SOC staff to respond to alerts generated by this use case*
2					
3					
4					

Table 5.1: Use case log book sample

However, consider table 5.1 only as a starting point and you may want to add much more information in the log book. Some examples are as follows:

1. Use case author

2. Date and time of creation/implementation

3. Modification history

You may also want to keep a *"wish list"* of new use cases that SOC team would like to implement with a priority associated with each item in the wish list.

5.4.4 Use Case Examples

Developing and maintaining use cases is a science and art. What should be the *right set of use cases* for your organization is completely depends upon your risk profiles. However, there is plenty of information available from different sources to help you pick and choose from [5][17][23].

- Insider Threat - Detection of suspicious activity resulting from actions of insiders.

- Data Exfiltration - Check if a data is being exfiltrated from your organization.

- Compliance - Use cases for compliance with different industry standards or government regulations like HIPAA, SOX, PCI DSS and others.

- Brute Force Attacks - Detection of brute force attacks against identity and access management systems or other valuable data sources.

- Ransomware Attacks - Early detection of any ransomware activity.

- Missing Logs - A use case to detect if any log source stopped sending log data. This happens more frequently than we would like to see it.

One key aspect of selecting use cases is not the *quantity or number* of use cases but the *quality* of detection rules and availability of telemetry data to enable effectiveness of detection.

5.5 Vulnerability Scanning

Outcome of SQL injection attack on a database server that is vulnerable for such attacks is very different than the outcome of an attack on a different server which is not vulnerable. Understanding existing vulnerabilities and making them part of correlation is crucial to assign severity of an event and urgency to respond to it. For this reason, ongoing scanning of network and application vulnerabilities and importing vulnerability data into SIEM is crucial.

Although this is not a text on vulnerability management, a typical vulnerability management lifecycle is shown in Figure 5.3. It is a continuous and on-going work that has to be repeated with established frequency.

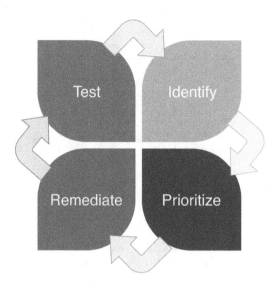

Figure 5.3: Vulnerability Management Lifecycle

Most of the modern SIEM tools have options for importing vulnerability scanning data and use it for correlation and enrich the alerting confidence level. However, when selecting SIEM technology and vulnerability scanning tools, make sure these are compatible with each other.

Attack Penetration Testing and Red Teaming Exercises: Going beyond vulnerability scanning.

Attack and penetration testing goes a step beyond vulnerability scanning by trying to exploit identified vulnerabilities. Sometimes it may be a good idea to combine vulnerability scanning with penetration testing, at least once a year.

Red Team Exercises are getting more popularity as they are very useful in identifying gaps in SOC capabilities to detect threats. Although this text is not about vulnerability management program, my suggestion is to use a combination of vulnerability scanning, penetration testing, and red team exercises throughout the year.

5.5.1 Asset Discovery and Asset Management

Maintaining a *comprehensive* assets database is crucial both for SOC as well as for vulnerability scanning. You cannot manage the vulnerability of the inventory, software and services you don't know you have. Many vulnerability scanners are also able to perform asset discovery but are not always accurate, depending upon network segmentation and host configurations.

A Configuration Management Database (CMDB) is typically used for proper asset management. Strong IT Service Management (ITSM) processes provide a good baseline for effective vulnerability management.

5.5.2 Network Vulnerability Scanning

Network vulnerability scanning is a very old security task and most security professionals are familiar with tools and techniques used for network vulnerability scanning. As new vulnerabilities are discovered, ongoing update of these tools and repeated scanning is necessary. The real question is how often vulnerability scanning should occur? Most standards require this at least once-a-quarter. However, many organizations perform vulnerability scanning on weekly or monthly basis. The idea is to fix crucial vulnerabilities as early as possible and test the fixes with a second scanning. At the same time you don't want it to be too frequent such that it become disruptive to normal business operations. Consider the following:

1. Create a tiered approach where critical assets are scanned more frequently. One approach could be scanning a small subset consisting of critical assets on weekly basis whereas a general network scanning once a month.

2. Vulnerability scanning is only as good as asset management. If you don't have correct inventory of assets, you will miss critical vulnerabilities that could be exploited by attackers.

3. Make vulnerability scanning comprehensive, including on-premises and Cloud.

4. Cloud-based tools for vulnerability are available and usually need less maintenance. Updating scanning tools is crucial for effective scanning.

5. *Prioritization* of identified vulnerabilities is an essential part of network vulnerability scanning. Just sending scan output to IT teams for remediation will be very poor practice and will create unnecessary overhead for others.

Caution: Don't Kill Production Systems

Some older systems and application may respond poorly to vulnerability scanning tools, causing systems to crash or become unresponsive. A common practice is to require a test scan in non-production environments to identify any issues like that. Some vulnerability scanning systems also categorize *safe scan* options.

If you are using a hosting service or a Cloud service, check your contracts with the vendors. Some vendors do require advance notification before you conduct vulnerability scanning.

With migration to the Cloud, many organizations have hybrid networks with some systems hosted by a Cloud Service Provider whereas other hosted in private data centers. The network vulnerability scanning should be able to cover both private network as well as Cloud infrastructure.

5.5.3 Web Application Vulnerability Scanning

Public web applications are a major and attractive target of attacks as they can provide access to back-end systems and data through the public Internet. While some vulnerabilities are easy to find (e.g. SQL injection and Cross Site Scripting), others may be related to logical flaws that need more than just vulnerability scanning tools. Expert web application vulnerability testers are needed to find these types of flaws.

A strategy for managing web application vulnerability may be different than managing network and operating system vulnerabilities. In some cases, organizations may not have option to modify web applications and instead rely on web application firewalls (WAF) as a workaround to hide web application vulnerabilities from potential attackers. A zero trust network architecture is also effective in hiding web application vulnerabilities that can't be immediately fixed (ZTNA).

5.5.4   Mobile Application Vulnerability Scanning

More and more businesses are using mobile apps and integrating these apps into back-end data sources. Managing vulnerabilities of mobile apps is a becoming increasingly important as mobile app use grows. Mobile apps also have additional challenges related to authentication, transient data saved on mobile devices, among others.

From a human behavior perspective, studies show that people are more likely to trust mobile devices and would click more often on URLs than they would on desktops. This makes them more susceptible and adds a new dimension to effectively managing mobile vulnerabilities.

5.5.5   Wireless LAN Vulnerability Scanning

Wi-Fi networks vulnerability assessment is a field in itself and should not be ignored. Many systems are available to continuously scan wireless networks as well as detect rogue wireless access points.

5.5.6   Endpoints, laptops vulnerability scanning

Vulnerability scanning for end points using traditional network vulnerability scanning methods has been a challenge. These devices are usually not always ON or connected to network, may be mobile, and typically use IP addresses provided by DHCP servers. Newer EDR tools with options to perform vulnerability scanning on the device itself are quite useful in tracking vulnerabilities on endpoints. Although selection of EDR tools may be outside the SOC scope, a close collaboration among IT teams can help achieve effective vulnerability management and strength SOC operations.

5.6   What about SOAR?

Security Orchestration, Automation and Response (SOAR) is a common name referred to technologies that enable security operations to collect and analyze information using both machine and human resources and automate digital workflows to respond to event [18]. Many vendors provide these technologies that integrate into SIEM and enable carrying out automated tasks in the form of playbooks.

SOAR technology, if implemented properly, can bring significant value in the form of time saving and SOC analyst satisfaction by eliminating mundane work. Like other technologies, SOAR solutions should also be researched and implemented carefully to get full value from investment. A key aspect of successful SOAR implementation is integration with other security systems and creating playbooks.

5.6.1   Do I Need SOAR?

While SOAR brings efficiency, automation, and analyst satisfaction, it may be overkill in some small SOC implementations where you have very few actionable events/incidents on a daily basis. I have heard from a number of practitioners that purchase and effective implementation of SOAR technologies is not only cost prohibitive, but also require an increase in payroll to maintain it. In some cases, you may be better off using scripts to implement some automation instead of going for a sophisticated solution. Remember, more technologies is not always a good thing!

5.6.2 Other Means for Automation

While providing automation is one of the primary objective of SOAR, you don't have to have a SOAR platform to do automated response. It helps, for sure, but it can be done on a system running Python scripts just as well. Many SOAR platforms run everything as Pythons scripts anyway.

5.7 Behavioral Analysis, UBA, UEBA

In addition to implementing typical use cases, identifying behavior patterns could provide clues to suspicious activity, whether for individual users or machines (entities). Many times these technologies that identify these patterns are referred to as *"User Behavior Analysis"* (UBA), or *User and Entity Behavior Analysis* (UEBA). Effective UEBA implementation also depends upon integration with other systems like asset management and identity management.

Some SIEM vendors have UEBA technologies already integrated into SIEM whereas in other cases you can have a separate technology implemented for a specific purpose. Modern anomaly detection methods like machine learning are a key differentiator in effectively detecting suspicious behavior.

In addition to log data, telemetry from networks (netflow data or pcap data) can also provide indications to behavior analysis, misconfigurations and anomalies. Many times anomalies detected using UEBA are basis for threat hunting activities.

While selecting tools for behavioral analysis, you should consider the following:

- Does the technology requires an agent to be installed on endpoints?
- Does it correctly identify a user or machine?
- Can it self learn and re-baseline without human intervention?
- Does it integrate into your SIEM technology or need a separate dashboard?
- Does it connect into Cloud and SaaS applications?
- Can you configure any known exceptions?

For these technologies, it may not be a bad idea to invite some vendors to demo their solutions to your team and build a selection criteria based upon what you learn from these presentations.

> Beyond UBA, UEBA, analytics is the future for effective threat detection. Correlation can't keep up with the levels of sophistication of attackers and evasion methods. We must strive to allow machines to do the analytics and then watch log/instrumentation streams near real-time and react.

5.8 Incident Lifecycle Management

Incident lifecycle management is part of many security standards and practices published by NIST, ISO, and others. A good incident response starts with incident response planning and preparation with an objective of quickly identifying and responding to incidents, and reducing number of incidents in the long run by focusing on fixing the root causes and improving resilience of IT systems.

NIST SP 800-61 [20] describes 4 phases of incident lifecycle plan as listed below and shown in Figure 5.4.

- Preparation

- Detection and analysis

- Containment, eradication and recovery

- Post-incident activities

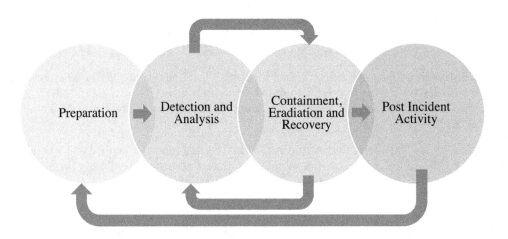

Figure 5.4: NIST 800-61 incident management lifecycle

The ISO 27035 standard outlines five stages of an incident lifecycle management as listed below, which are similar to NIST.

- *Prepare* phase includes building incident management policy, procedures, response team.

- *Identify* phase includes combining tools, risk intelligence and human factors to identify incidents.

- *Assess* phase deals with prioritization and planning for remediation.

- *Respond* phase is about containing and remediating incidents and recover any systems that have been impacted.

- *Learn* phase is after-the-fact exercise of learning lessons from incidents, identifying root causes, and taking actions to stop similar incidents from happening in the future.

Other frameworks including COBIT [25] and ITIL [3] also provide recommendations for incident management and response. The key is to build a policy and procedures as a starting point by getting guidance from any framework or standard of your choice and then build a practice around it.

5.8.1 Ticketing System

When building an incident response plan, a system is needed to document incidents, assigning priorities, assigning tasks, and managing overall workflow. Many organizations prefer to use a ticketing system similar to something that other IT teams use. If you plan to leverage an organization-wide ticketing system, care must be taken to ensure sensitive security incident data is not accessible to other teams who don't have a need-to-know. This is not an easy task as the ticketing systems have reports and dashboards, access for developers and support staff which makes it difficult to put stringent controls. For those reasons, some organizations decide to use a ticketing/incident management system specific to the SOC which enables access to only SOC staff. However, there are pros and cons of both approaches. Please note that if there is a budget constraint, an open source tools could be helpful. I have even witnessed the use of spreadsheets to track incidents, which may work but is not necessarily a good practice due to issues of scalability, data integrity/currency, and document control. The ticketing system must have a workflow component to ensure the lifecycle of security incidents is properly managed.

5.8.2 Knowledge Management

SOC analysts always find tips and tricks while dealing with incidents, especially where there are exceptions or idiosyncrasies related to an organization. Knowledge management tools are very handy to document these for broader SOC team to take advantage of. Many times, managing a knowledge base is part of job description of tier II and tier III SOC analysts.

Once again both commercial and open source tools are available for knowledge management. A typical wiki solution would work in many cases.

5.9 IT Foundation Stack

Many of the SOC technologies mentioned earlier use IT foundation for operations. Popular SIEM platforms run on servers that require standard IT processes and procedures. Similarly log collection and storage rely on network and storage systems. Fundamentally, when building SOC, you need to build a strong partnership with other IT and network teams who will enable the underlying technologies.

5.9.1 Network Support for SOC

The network is a key foundation for SOC with following considerations:

- You need logs from many network devices. In many organizations, managing firewalls, VPN, proxies and other functions may be a shared responsibility between network and security teams.

- Log data collection over network could be a significant impact on the network capacity, especially if you are using a Cloud based SIEM solution.

- SOC will be on a segmented network and you need help to design and implement this segment.

- For adding new log sources, you will need help in change management and planning for network bandwidth.

For these and other reasons, network teams are a key partner in successful SOC implementation and smooth operations. Most of the time, the network team is also part of incident response and works closely with the SOC team.

5.9.2   Operating Systems Management

A number of SOC systems requires servers, desktops and other end-user devices that require continuous patching and updates. Although managing operating systems is not a core SOC function, you have to build a partnership with other teams to achieve your goals.

5.9.3   Storage

Storage planning is key to keeping logs for a specific period of time to meet compliance needs as well as to aid in forensic. At minimum you would need two types of storage, one for online and high speed log retrieval and search capability and another one to store archived data for longer periods of time.

If you plan to go with a cloud based SIEM solution, storage will be a little easier to manage in the Cloud but still needs proper planning.

5.10   Forensic and Other Tools

Forensic investigations is a key SOC function. More than tools, retaining expertise and talent for investigations may be an even more costly proposition, especially if forensic investigation is not a daily task (which is the case for most of the small to medium implementation of SOC). For that reason, many organizations maintain a basic capability and outsource in-depth investigations to third parties on as-needed basis.

For large companies, it may make sense to hire forensic investigators where the kind and degree of investigative needs warrant it. For smaller organizations, outsourcing makes more sense.

Use of Kali Linux is popular as it provides many forensic investigation tools as well as vulnerability assessment and network penetration testing. The distributions could be a friend of first responders. Many commercial tools are available for forensic investigations as well.

5.11   Reporting and Dashboards

Finding the right metrics that accurately show performance of SOC and then automating these metrics is not an easy task. Many organizations struggle with good metrics and reporting. At the basic level, you need to have at least:

- **Executive level metrics** and dashboards and reporting to show what *business value* SOC is creating for the company.

- **Technical reports and dashboards** to help SOC and other technology teams measure their progress on resolving issues.

The more focus you put on reporting during the planning phase, the greater the likelihood of success of your reporting. Reporting and dashboards can be modified on an as need basis afterwards. Focus first on constructing a basic set of reports and dashboards with high quality and relevance. You can, of course, continue to build on this foundation going forward as needs are defined and evolve.

5.12   Technology Integration

Just like the right tools and technology are necessary, integration of the tools is even more important. At minimum, take steps to assure that the following integration points are implemented at some level.

1. Vulnerability management systems and SIEM

2. Asset management with corporate IT asset management systems

3. SIEM and ticketing system such that SIEM noticeable events are able to create tickets for further follow up

4. SOAR needs a number of integration points with internal as well as external technologies

5. UEBA requires integration into identity and access management as well as asset management

5.13 Summary of Technologies, Capabilities and Services

Table 5.2 shows a list of technologies, capabilities and services needed for different levels of SOC maturity and/or size. If you just started building a new SOC, start with foundational level even if you plan to build a large SOC eventually.

SOC Type	List of tools, capabilities and practices
Foundational needs for small or new SOC	• **Tools** - SIEM, log collection, vulnerability scanning, incident response lifecycle, Wiki for knowledge management, ticketing system, asset discovery and asset management, a Linux distribution with basic security tools (e.g. Kali Linux) • **Capabilities** - Incident response, use case creation and fine tuning • **Practices** - Regular mock incident table top exercises, metrics, dashboards and reports
Mature SOC operations	• **Tools** - SOAR, forensic tools, UEBA/UBA • **Capabilities** - threat intelligence integration into SIEM and other security technologies • **Practices** - Red teaming exercises
Advanced SOC, large SOC	• **Tools** - full packet capture analysis, NetFlow data collection and analysis • **Capabilities** - weather and other news feeds displays for situational awareness • **Practices** - threat hunting, membership of relevant ISAC and information sharing

Table 5.2: SOC Technology Priorities

Also, please note that information in table 5.2 is a recommendation and you may choose a different approach for your particular situation. The important aspect of planning is that there must be a good thought process about different phases of SOC implementation and tools/technologies needed for each phase.

5.14   Chapter Summary and Recommendations

- Research and planning for required SOC technologies can save a lot of trouble down the road. You can take advantage of your vendors with tools like *Request for Information (RFI)* to understand available SOC technology options.

- Many SOC technologies have inter-dependency. For example, when choosing a vulnerability management tool, make sure its output can be directly imported into the SIEM solution. If you are using a managed security services provider (MSSP), check with the MSSP which vulnerability scanning tools they support.

- A large number of open source technologies are available to build SOC. The trade-off is between ease of use and cost. You may spend significant cost in implementing open source technologies whereas commercial packages may provide quick implementation and ease of use.

- Always start with threat modeling before building use cases. Document scenarios that are more relevant to your particular situation, identify threat actors, their methods of attack and how an attack will manifest in logs. Only then start building use cases. Enabling default SIEM use cases is a common mistake that wastes significant time for SOC staff.

- No SOC is built in isolation and you need partnership with broader IT teams to implement and operate foundational technologies including but not limited to networking, operating systems, desktops and so on.

- If possible, keep SOC incident management systems and processes isolated from broader IT ticketing systems to safeguard against accidental disclosure of confidential data. However, you may want to use IT ticketing system for remediation tasks.

- Look for opportunities where you can outsource less-commonly-used SOC functions like forensics. This can reduce overall cost and better optimization of SOC operations.

- Vulnerability management systems are as good as asset management processes. A flawed asset management process will result in unpatched systems with unknown vulnerabilities that eventually will be exploited by attackers.

— If you don't know where you are going, you will get nowhere
— Planning makes future more predictable not sure why people still don't do it.

Anonymous

6

SOC Implementation Planning

When Joanna got budget approval for building security operations center, she and her team at a large media company were absolutely thrilled. As CISO, she had been fighting for this budget to build SOC for last two years. Finally, the company board of directors realized the need for better management of their risk after being hit by a ransomware attack.

The team worked with vendors to acquire software tools and a Cloud-based SIEM solution for a faster implementation. The Cloud based solution came with a promise of scalability and would enable them get more storage if and when needed. The initial testing of sending log data to Cloud-based SIEM and generating alerts worked very well. However, as they started adding more log sources from different office locations and data centers, they soon realized that their network did not have enough bandwidth to send large amounts of log at three out of seven locations. They started working with their internal network team to increase bandwidth at these locations but the network team manager informed that they were busy in other projects and this project was not on their priority list. With some escalations, Joanna was able to bring the network team on-board and and request their Internet Service Provider (ISP) for additional bandwidth. It took the ISP two more months to serve the request causing significant delay to complete the initial phase of SOC project.

Not all SOC projects are very smooth or even as successful as the above fictional story shows. Most of the failed SOC projects don't fail because of budget or technology or financial resources, but because of poor planning. Failure to understand project dependencies, capacity of an organization to absorb amount of change, dependencies on other corporate projects, and poor project planning are key reasons for less-than optimal SOC implementations. There is no such thing as *too soon* time for starting project planning. Once you have an organizational buy-in, start the planning process immediately. Initial planning should actually be part of your business case.

Most of the discussion in this chapter is focused on creating and executing a project plan for successful SOC implementation with a focus on plan, design, and build. Typically a project manager will play a key role in building SOC plan and then execute it. There is a good likelihood that the project manager may not be very familiar with building SOC and this chapter will provide a good starting point for him/her about the work and dependencies. The objective is to make sure that any major part of the project is not missed in the project plan.

6.1   Plan, Design, Build and Operate

Conceptually you should always keep in mind different phases of overall SOC initiative. The focus of this chapter is on planning, designing and building the SOC. Typically, SOC operations starts when you have completed building and handed it over to the steady state operations team. Three circles on the left hand side of figure 6.1 shows phases of the overall SOC project that should be part of project planning.

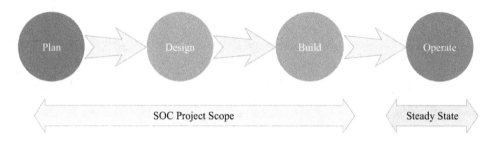

Figure 6.1: SOC Project Scope

To expedite the process, you could engage an experienced service provider to help you do plan, design, and build parts and then use your internal team to operate SOC on an ongoing basis. However, keep in mind that creating policies, procedures and testing is still part of the "build" phase. For example, you will test incident response processes in the build phase to make sure all components and technologies needed for incident response are in place before SOC enters into steady state. Some service providers can also co-operate the SOC with your team for a specified period before handing over the complete operational responsibility to your internal team.

6.2   Do I Need a Project Manager?

Formal engagement of a project manager is a good practice for any sizable project. Project managers are trained in using standard project management methodologies including work breakdown, resource management, financial discipline and to ensure that project succeeds in achieving its objectives and a timely completion. Many organizations have project management office (PMO) to run internal projects in a professional manner. For organizations with an established PMO, one or more project managers are usually assigned to approved projects. Even if you have PMO, there is a possibility that you may not have a project manager for the initial planning until the SOC project is formally approved.

For the initial pre-approval phase, you don't need a formal project manager as long as someone can take that role and understands fundamentals of project planning, including but not limited to, creating tasks, assigning task owners, setting target dates, task tracking, and managing project budget. A sound project plan is crucial for success of SOC project, as SOC implementation usually has dependencies on many other technology teams.

When creating project plan for SOC, make sure to consider the following.

- A successful project plan needs a project manager and use of a standard project management methodology (e.g. established by Project Management Institute or PMI[1]).

- Always divide project into smaller and manageable phases that span no more than 6 months each. The shorter, the better.

- Devise a mechanism to measure outcome of each phase.

- Have your best technology architects design the solution and conduct peer reviews for the architecture. Spending time in planning and designing could save significant trouble down the road during the implementation.

- Identify all dependencies of the SOC project. For example, collecting logs from servers needs work from the server team that may have environment freeze for certain months of the year.

- Review your project plan with all IT teams who have any dependency and think about alternatives.

If you are engaging a service provider for SOC implementation, typically they will have their own project manager. However, you may still need an internal project manager to align internal resources for successful completion of your project.

6.3 Project Lifecycle

Project Management Institute (PMI) has published project management body of knowledge (PMBOK) that is basis of methodologies most of the organizations have adopted. According to PMBOK, the project lifecycle is divided into five major groups or phases as listed below.

1. **Initiation** - In this phase you will define the project, its charter and scope, assign a project manager, assemble team.

2. **Planning** - In this phase you will create a project plan, break projects into smaller tasks, estimate work needed for each task, create timeline, and owners of tasks.

3. **Execution** - The main tasks for execution is to manage tasks and teams, ensure timeline for different tasks is met.

4. **Monitoring and Controlling** - Manage dependencies for the project, manage and control cost, manage risk, manage resources, resolve any issues impacting project timeline.

5. **Closing** - Ensure all tasks are complete and project objectives are met. Do closing and "lessons learned" meeting. Hand off the project to steady state operations teams.

These phases are also shows in Figure 6.2. Many times you have a multi-phase project where you will close one phase and initiate the next phase of the project and this can continue in a cycle.

As you can see all of these stages of project management are crucial for a successful build of SOC. However, keep in mind that all projects are time-bound and have a start and an end point (closing). This essentially means that when SOC is built, the project ends and a steady state operations start where SOC team is taking input data, identifying incidents and responding to incidents (among other tasks). The steady state operations will be the topic of the next chapter.

---

[1] https://www.pmi.org/

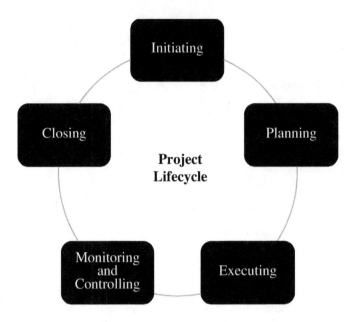

Figure 6.2: Project Lifecycle

The next parts of this chapter includes some important components of your overall project plan.

6.4   SOC Logistics

Logistics for a SOC project are numerous and are an important part of project plan. Logistics include everything outside of the technology stack discussed in Chapter 5. For example, SOC location, furniture etc. Important logistic items are listed in this section but there could be more. I would suggest creating a separate section in the project plan for logistics with detailed work breakdown and task assignments. Depending upon the type of your SOC project and its scope, this section may be very small or quite long.

CAUTION

Many people don't understand or downplay the role of these logistics for the success of the SOC project and are highly focused on the technology and SOC processes. It is not a bad thing but keep in mind that proper logistics are also a crucial part of achieving SOC objectives and managing budget.

6.4.1   Physical Location for SOC

Physical location matters significantly for various reasons. Make the following as part of your project plan.

- Decide where the technology (servers, storage, etc.) will be hosted. For large organizations and distributed environment, technology could be installed in multiple locations. With modern technologies, some part of the SOC technology stack may be in the Cloud. Also "where" matters since floorspace in a data center, rack, and power have different costs in different regions. If SOC infrastructure is hosted in Cloud, then costs in this case may not matter as much.

- Location where SOC people come to work may be different than where the technology is installed. For global organizations, you may have multiple SOC locations in follow-the-sun model.

- If you plan to have forensic lab, you may need special location with specific controls to ensure proper protection of evidence.

- While deciding location, consider availability of talent/qualified people needed to run SOC. This would also have significant impact on the operational cost of SOC. Payroll is quite different for various geographical locations because of cost of living.

- Any compliance needs for storing data in specific geographic locations as more and more countries mandate that data of their citizens does not leave specific regions or geographical boundaries of a country.

- Also consider business continuity and find a place that is away from potential of natural disasters.

Sometimes proximity to other IT teams is also a considerations. If you are building a virtual SOC where people can work from anywhere, location for people may not matter that much but location for the SOC technology infrastructure still matters.

6.4.2 Furniture and Physical Storage

For virtual SOC, furniture probably would not matter that much. However, many SOC operations have physical locations so you may want to consider furniture needs. Make the following part of your project plan.

- Trivial furniture items like chairs, tables, cabinets, etc.

- For forensic labs, evidence collection and evidence storage, you will need specific types of locked storage. Pay special attention to this as the requirements may be different depending upon where the SOC is (depending upon country laws).

- Arranging a small sofa would not be a bad idea. There is a lot of stress that SOC analysts go through and you need to find a way to relax a little.

The furniture should be comfortable and electronics friendly with options for managing power and network cables.

6.4.3 Computers, Laptops, Printers, etc.

While these items are still related to technology, I consider these logistics as these are not part of the SOC technology stack described in Chapter 5. Consider these as utility machines that SOC staff would use, sometimes on adhoc basic and sometime permanently. These technologies are useful for installing and using different tools for vulnerability management, forensics and other purposes. Make the following part of your project plan as basic needs for analysts.

- For all SOC analysts, laptops with encrypted storage must be required (full disk encryption). Plan for large memory and storage for these laptops in case analysts need to run resource-heavy tools or virtual machines.

- Other equipment will be needed for taking disk images, running forensic tools, case management and so on.

- Write-block devices are necessary for taking images of physical disks.

- Printers, paper shredders, storage media destruction tools.

Consider the above as "supporting technology" for SOC. The larger the scope of the SOC, the more support technology is required.

6.4.4   Network Bandwidth and Internet Connectivity

Network is crucial part for multiple reasons. First of all you need enough network bandwidth to collect all log and other telemetry data. You also need good network connectivity for SOC staff for research. Make the following part of your project plan.

- Plan for adequate network capacity required to collect log data. As the data always grows over time, it would be better to plan for more bandwidth than the actual estimates of your log volume. In case SIEM is hosted in the Cloud, you may be less concern about the bandwidth in the Cloud. However, you still need to send logs to the Cloud so extra bandwidth will be needed.

- Redundant network is almost always required for uninterrupted flow of log data.

- Acquiring extra network bandwidth on-premise does need some time, sometime in months. Planning ahead for this will help. Consult with your network team and they will be able to give you a good estimate of time required to get extra bandwidth, based upon their previous experiences with the network providers.

Sometimes it may be tempting to bring a broadband connection to the SOC for research purposes but it could have other unintended consequences and implications. As an example, it opens up door for unintentional sharing of SOC information outside the organization, bridging networks, etc.

6.4.5   TV Display Screens

Well sometimes you want to make your SOC look a little "cool" to people visiting it! Who does not like TV screens with blinking lights or scrolling information. But seriously, adding some video display screens can be quite useful. You can consider having multiple TV screens to continuously display information relevant to SOC operations. Plan for the number, function, and placement of these TV screen monitors, including but not limited to the following and make it part of your project plan.

- High risk alerts that your analysts should be or are working on.

- Weather conditions to keep you updated about what is happening at different business locations. Sometimes this information factors into incident response activities.

- Breaking news from reliable new sources - This could help take proactive measures if there is a widespread virus/worm outbreak and a vulnerability that could have major impact on SOC operations.

- Important stock tickers information may be quite useful for some SOC operations in specific industries.

- If you are going to receive TV signal through a satellite, you have to look into installing dish antennas and cabling which may be a challenge in some scenarios of high-rise buildings. Otherwise, plan to receive TV signal via cable or over the Internet.

The project plan should include the sources of this information and how to make these sources available to SOC.

6.5 Implementing the Technology Stack

Once you have finalized the location where the SOC technology will be installed, it is time to start planning for implementation. A detailed project plan that takes into account dependencies is crucial.

Make the following part of your project plan.

- Consider technology procurement and support contract details. Your procurement organization and legal team is usually involved in finalizing contracts with outside vendors. The project plan should allocate enough time to go through legal and contracting phases, which could be quite long.

- Other than equipment, also consider professional services from vendors for the implementation.

- Typically, you have to install technology at multiple locations. Data storage and analytics stack could be at one central location or multiple location for larger implementations.

- Some systems may be installed on-premises whereas others could be in the Cloud. For example, you may have on-premises SIEM solution whereas vulnerability management in the cloud (e.g. a SaaS service).

- **Log Collection** stack may be distributed where you will have log collection servers (log collectors) at each location that collect local log data and send it to a central location.

Log and other telemetry data collection is one of the main part of implementation. Refer to Chapter 3 for detailed discussion about log collection infrastructure.

6.5.1 Log collection

Make the following part of your project plan.

- Decide and plan for important log sources.

- Plan for number and location of local log collectors.

- Estimate network bandwidth requirements for log forwarding. In some cases you may need to add network bandwidth.

6.5.2 Netflow Collection and Analysis

Netflow is an important source of threat identification and anomaly detection. Plan for:

- Strategic locations in your network to collect netflow data.

- Software to store and analyze the netflow data.

- Machine learning for detecting anomalies.

- Tools for netflow data analysis.

- Integration into SIEM.

6.5.3 Raw Packet Capture

Raw packet data is very helpful in investigations even if it is not processed in the normal business situations in real time. Many tools exist to both capture and analyze raw packet data. In case of a data breach, investigators can use this data to replay network traffic and trace back what happened in the past. Typically, keeping 30 days worth of packet capture should provide decent window into the past, although it may not be sufficient for data breaches older than that period of time. The project plan should include:

- Strategic locations where packet capture will be done.

- Procurement of necessary hardware, like network taps.

- Server and ample storage to capture network data and store it. Sometimes compressing data and storing in the Cloud could be quite helpful and cost effective.

- Tools to analyze data if and when needed.

6.5.4   Plan for Storage Needs

You will need storage in multiple scenarios and storage capacity planning may include the following:

- Primary storage for online log data.

- Secondary storage for storing archive data.

- Explore options for archive data in the Cloud and in some situations it may make sense.

- Storage for data other than logs (e.g. Netflow, Network capture data).

6.5.5   Ticketing and Workflow Management

A ticketing system is needed for managing incident lifecycle, change management requests. In your project plan, include procurement, installation, and training of staff for managing tickets.

6.5.6   Forensics and Investigation

Forensic and investigations require proper handling of evidence. Include software and hardware tools as well as evidence handling facilities with proper chain of custody plans.

6.6   People Planning

Qualified people are the most crucial part of SOC. Make the following as part of your SOC project plan:

- **Operations Time:** 24x7, 8x5, or other

- Number of people required

- Roles and skills definition

- Job descriptions

- When to advertise for jobs and start hiring? Is there a progressive plan to start small and then grow the team?

- Career progression paths

Refer to Chapter 4 for detailed discussion about human resources.

6.7 Business Continuity and Disaster Recovery (BC/DR)

Business Continuity and Disaster Recovery (BC/DR) for SOC is an essential part of SOC planning. Following are some key areas to include in the SOC plan:

- Familiarize yourself with BC/DR principles such as Recovery Time Objectives and Recovery Point Objectes (RTO/RPO)[2].

- Define business continuity and recovery objectives, time constraints.

- Based upon the objectives, include how SOC will recover from disasters and continue operations in the case of a disaster.

- The plan should include:
  - Location and systems for alternate operations center.
  - People and communications plans.
  - Data backup and recovery.

- In many cases, splitting the SOC into two locations that act as backup of each other could be a decent strategy.

> **Implication of BC/DR on SOC design**
>
> Requirements for business continuity and disaster recovery will drive your desing for SOC implementation. For example, you may decide to have multiple physical locations for your SOC technology stack. Similarly you may also want to send logs to more than one locations or opt for real-time replication of SIEM data to disaster recovery site.

6.8 Building Policies, Procedures, and Standards

Part of the project plan must include creating policies, procedures and standards for SOC operations. Common SOC policies, procedures, plan must include:

- Incident identification, escalation and response
- Log collection
- Change management
- Forensic
- Data encryption, storage, aging, and retrieval
- Device hardening
- Vulnerability management
- Business continuity and disaster recovery
- Human resources
- Managing operational shifts
- Training and continuous development
- Threat intelligence

---

[2]https://en.wikipedia.org/wiki/Disaster_recovery

If this sounds like a lot of work, it is. However, it is necessary to have this work done before SOC testing and closing the project. The operations team will rely on these policies, procedures and standards to effectively run the SOC.

6.9   Performance Metrics and Reports

How would you measure performance of SOC and if it is meeting the business objectives? Creating reliable and meaningful metrics are necessary for the project plan.

Also make sure that most of the metrics and reports are automated otherwise it becomes a cumbersome manual task which may introduce errors.

6.10   Governance Model

In the project plan, create SOC governance model. Section 2.13 describes considerations for building a SOC governance model, stakeholders and their duties. Make sure the governance model is reviewed and/or approved by all stakeholders as part of your project plan.

6.11   SOC Testing

Testing is usually the last part of the SOC project plan before handing it over to the steady state operations team. The project must ensure all SOC technologies, processes, metrics and reporting work correctly. SOC testing should include many tests for quality controls, including but not limited to:

- Log ingestion in different scenarios with disruption in network availability.
- Testing for disaster recovery and business continuity.
- Testing of each policy and procedure to ensure they work in real world scenarios.
- Incident response process testing, which may include many sub-tests.
- Testing performance metrics and reporting.

Make sure the project plan includes a formal "sign off" on test results and formal acceptance from stakeholders.

6.12   Project Closing

Last but not the least, the project plan must include steps for closing the project which could include:

- A formal acceptance of SOC project completion by all stakeholders.
- Formal hand off to SOC operations team that includes:
  - Copies of policies, standards and procedures.
  - Testing results.
  - System user accounts, passwords or any other information to properly run SOC technology.
  - A formal meeting to discuss "lessons learned".

    – If SOC has multiple phases, discuss starting next phase and project team

Once the project is closed, the project team's work should end and the SOC operations team should take it over from that point onwards.

6.13 Chapter Summary and Recommendations

Although it may seem counter intuitive to some,spending time on project planning for SOC implementation will ultimately save time and shorten the length of project. Following are some key recommendations for SOC planning.

- Any successful project requires a detailed project planning. SOC is no exception to this.

- A SOC plan must include not only the initial implementation of technology, but also governance, processes, and metrics for ongoing operations.

- A typical SOC project includes collaboration across IT teams and has many dependencies outside the security operations. Failure to take these into account could severely impact success of SOC project

- Dividing the overall project into multiple smaller phases can improve chances of success as well as help you correct the course in case changes are needed along the way.

- SOC testing is a very crucial part of SOC planning to ensure everything works the way it should work. Test results must be formally accepted by all stakeholders before SOC is transitions to steady state operations team.

—SOC is a dynamic, fast paced, and a stressful work environment. While tools and technology play an important role, the real key to a successful SOC is people with a positive mindset.

anonymous

7

SOC Operations and Incident Response

In Chapter 6 section 6.1, I introduced Plan-Design-Build-Operate approach of the overall SOC project[1]. While the previous chapters have been about the planning, designing and building the SOC, this chapter is focused on steady state operations, governance, and carrying out SOC tasks efficiently.

Note that the steady state operations phase starts when the *SOC project* is finished, marking the completion of SOC *build* phase. Later in this book, under Part III, you will learn more about continuous improvement and, potentially, SOC scope enhancements as part of your multi-phase plan.

What we cover in this chapter includes:

- SOC governance

- Human Resource management

- Incident Detection and Response

- Managing SOC technology infrastructure

- Build and Improve use cases

- Dealing with SOC staff stress and burnout

- SOC reporting and metrics

- SOC and meeting compliance needs

- SOC best practices and pitfalls

This chapter is the culmination of all preparations and work you have been doing in previous chapters, resulting in realization of the goal you started with. Now is the time to ensure that

---

[1]Well, there is *"Improve"* and *"Expand"* phases as shown in Figure 1.3 but we are not considering those phases yet!

SOC performs its functions and achieves its business objectives to quickly identify and respond to security incidents.

7.1 SOC Governance

SOC team needs alliances and cooperation across the business and technology organization. Building a governance model plays a key role in building these alliances, proper functioning and day to day operations of SOC. Often, a good governance model is closely tied to even getting funding for SOC [10]. A good governance model is also necessary for continuous improvements and building scope for future SOC enhancements and securing funds.

The governance model provides business leaders an oversight mechanism for SOC strategy, operations, review SOC policies and processes, and to continuously evaluate effectiveness of SOC. Failure to put a governance structure will significantly decrease probability achieving SOC objectives. The following part of this section highlights some of the activities that need to be part of SOC governance.

7.1.1 SOC Governance Board

The purpose of the governance board is to provide oversight for SOC operations. Selection of member of the governance board starts with identifying stakeholders. Section 1.7 on page 10 shows a list of usual SOC stakeholders. However, there may be additional stakeholders in your organization who would be your partner in success and should be included in the board. When creating a governance board, please ensure that following considerations are taken into account:

1. Create a purpose, mission and responsibility document for the governance board.

2. Include at least one member from each stakeholder team.

3. Schedule periodic meetings of the governance board with specific agenda. Agenda items related to performance reports of SOC should be part of every meeting.

4. The board should approve any change or update to policies and procedures of SOC.

5. The board should ensure that SOC is meeting its objectives. If not, the board should recommend corrective actions.

6. Collaboration with broader technology teams (or lack of it) should be discussed in regular board meetings.

7. The board should also advise on future direction of SOC scope and SOC expansion as well as continuous improvement.

As you can see from the above list, the governance board is crucial for the success of SOC operations and making any adjustments that are required from time to time.

7.1.2 Create Policies, Procedures and Standards

Development of policies, standards and procedures should be part of the project plan as mentioned in section 6.8. This basically means that a majority of policies and procedures should be ready before SOC enters into the steady state operations phase. However, that is always not the case. You may have some of these documents but these may be in initial phases of development. Even for mature SOC, you always need to review and update policies and procedures as part of a regular governance process.

Table 7.1 shows a list of policies and procedures that are essential for running a SOC. While creating these policies and procedures, get help from overall corporate security policies and IT procedures to keep SOC policies consistent with corporate policies.

Category	List of Policies and Processes
Policies	• Change management policy • Incident management policy • Log management policy • Data encryption, storage, aging, and retrieval policies • Devices hardening policy • Vulnerability management policy • Business continuity and disaster recovery policy • Human resources policy • Threat intelligence gathering and use policy
Processes	• Change management process • Incident response process • Log management process • Incident identification, escalation and response process • Log collection process • Forensic process • Data storage, backup and retrieval process • Devices hardening process • Vulnerability management process • Business continuity and disaster recovery processes • Hiring processes • Managing operational shifts • Training and continuous development process • Threat intelligence gathering process • Threat intelligence integration process • Threat intelligence sharing process • Threat hunting process • Knowledge management process

Table 7.1: SOC Policies and Procedures

Keep policies and procedures simple and minimal so that each SOC staff member understands it. There is no need to write a PhD thesis that nobody fully understands, hence nobody fully follows.

When thinking about SOC processes, not only should you have good processes in place but also continuously evaluate process maturity and make continuous improvement. You can also take advantage of standards like COBIT, ISO 27K, ITIL and NIST to establish procedures.

While policies change less frequently, you may have to continuously learn from your operations and update your processes to make continuous improvements.

7.1.3   SOC Standards and Inclusion of Extended IT Teams

While many policies and processes would be used by the SOC staff, you should also create standards for the consumption of technology teams outside SOC. For example, infrastructure teams should know what they are supposed to do to enable logging for new servers or applications to be integrated into SOC. Similarly extended IT teams will be part of incident reporting and response processes. Some of the recommended standards for SOC are listed below.

- Log collection standards

- Incident identification and escalation standards

- Data encryption standards

If you have an internal GRC (Governance, Risk and Compliance) team, you can get help from their experts in creating effective policies, standards and processes.

7.1.4   Creating Process Flow Charts

Process flow charts are an effective way of creating a visualization of SOC processes. Swimlane charts enable you to add actors with process steps and decision making points. One of the advantages of creating process flow charts is that you can turn these flowcharts into posters that could be placed on walls for easy access to SOC staff and broader IT organization.

Once you have created swimlane flowcharts for a process, make sure to take it to the SOC governance board for approval before broader distribution. In fact, all policies, standards and processes must be approved by the SOC governance board.

7.1.5   External Relationships (Law Enforcement and Others)

There are multiple reasons you want to have established relationships with law enforcement agencies in your area. First of all, you may be *required* to report some incidents and data breaches to law enforcement. Secondly, in some cases, law enforcement agencies may actually inform you about a breach if you are a secondary victim/target by threat actors who are acting against others. Third, in case of a large scale incident, you may actually need law enforcement as part of your incident response plan to investigate the incident. Fourth, in some cases law enforcement agencies may have capabilities that you don't have in-house and can help you fill gaps. Last, but not the least, some cases may end up in a court of law and these agencies could help you preserve the evidence such that it is admissible in courts.

For these and many other reasons, it is wise to establish relationships proactively so that you don't scramble to find contacts in the time of need.

You may also want to have some relationships with print and broadcast media, although it may be through your internal public relationship organization. These relationships are very useful when you want to communicate to the general public or your customers in a meaningful and accurate manner as a response to a data breach.

7.1.6   Coordination with other Teams

The SOC governance board should help in establishing relationships, interfaces, and processes for interaction with other teams. These relationships are not only needed for effective incident response, but are also required for other SOC tasks. For example, the SOC needs to be aware of any network changes, new applications, changes to existing applications, subscription to Cloud services, adding or removing servers or software etc.

- Other IT teams may add new log sources that you would be interested in.

- Change in any policies and procedures need to be coordinated with broader technology teams.

- You may need to make changes to SOC infrastructure that would require support from IT teams.

- SOC business continuity and disaster recovery processes are also closely tied to support from other teams.

- In many cases you may also need help from legal, HR, procurement and other non-IT departments within your organization.

As you can imagine, the list shown above is very limited and there are other areas where coordination is necessary and required and should be made part of SOC governance.

7.1.7 Service Level Agreements (SLAs)

SLA are used to measure efficiency of any operation, whether it is IT, SOC, or anything else. The SLAs are designed to maintain a certain minimum level of service that SOC customers (other teams) can expect from SOC. The SLAs are published and must be measured and reported and should have association with the mission and objectives of the SOC [49]. You should also make sure that SLAs are reasonable so that SOC can actually meet but should not be too broad with no chances of failure.

Typical SOC SLAs include:

- SOC availability time and service hours.

- Time for incident identification to investigation.

- Time to escalation to CSIRT teams or incident responders.

- Mean time to resolution (MTTR).

- Mean time to onboard new log sources.

- Malware analysis

- Log retention and log retrieval

Note that in addition to SLAs for the SOC, you also need to make sure that any of your service providers also have defined SLAs and adhere to these. For examples, if you are outsourcing forensic or malware analysis to a third party, you must have SLAs signed with your service providers. If nothing else, you should have a support contract with your SIEM vendor that must include meaningful SLAs to make sure you get proper support when needed. When signing SLAs with your service providers, there should be a penalty when they fail to meet the SLAs.

7.2 Human Resource Management

From operations perspective, the main objective is to adequately man the SOC with an appropriate number of analysts in different shifts.

7.2.1   Schedules and Shifts for 24x7x365 Operations

When doing my research on SOC operations and talking to experienced SOC managers and CISOs, I found that there are multiple ways different companies are trying to manage shift operations. Some of there are mentioned below.

- *Nine Hour Shifts* are used where 24x7x365 SOC requires that an analyst working in one shift get half hour of overlap time with the previous and next shift to transfer the in-progress work to analysts in the next shift. There are three shifts in 24 hours with half hour overlap at the start and end of each shift.

- *Twelve Hour Shifts* work well in the scenario where SOC analysts work three days one week and four days the next week. This makes it easier to cover the weekends.

- *Rotation* is key to manage shifts so that analysts are not stuck in one specific shift.

- *Vacations and Emergencies* require that SOC managers work proactively with SOC staff to stagger vacation time such that the service is not disrupted.

Building an environment to reduce stress levels, nourish cooperation, creating a team spirit, and providing tools and technologies to enable SOC staff work effectively are some other key aspects to manage schedule and shifts.

7.2.2   Daily Calls and Touch Points

Keeping all SOC staff updated with activities is obviously important as many of the daily actions may be closely related to each other. Taking a scheduled time to connect everyone and share quick updates is very helpful. This is even more crucial for 24x7x365 at the start/end of every shift as mentioned earlier.

7.3   Incident Response Process

Incident detection and response is the most crucial process of a SOC. We have already seen NIST recommendations for incident lifecycle management in section 5.8 on page 63. While building your processes, you can further segment activities shown in Figure 5.4. For example, *Detection and Analysis* may be further divided into *Detect* and *Analyze* steps. Essentially, there are these following seven steps that emerge from expanding the diagram in Figure 5.4.

1. Prepare

2. Detect

3. Analyze

4. Contain

5. Eradicate

6. Recover

7. Post incident activities

The important thing is to have efficient processes in place to quickly detect and respond to incidents and shorten a recovery time.

7.3.1   Incident Response Playbooks

Incident response playbooks are typically used to define step-by-step processes for handling different types of incidents throughout the lifecycle. The playbooks could be in graphical format like flowcharts or swimlane diagrams as well in narrative formats.

Playbooks should reflect incident response policy and processes "in practice". You should also have a relationship of playbook with different use cases such that when an alert triggers, IR teams can quickly figure out which playbook to use/follow.

Some example of typical playbooks for a SOC may include:

- Virus outbreak

- Phishing attacks

- Ransomware

- Denial of service

- Website compromise

- IoT

Each playbook should include all steps in the NIST incident response process (unless you are using a different incident response process). You can get help from many online resources to build playbooks [8][48][2][4][31].

7.3.2   Internal vs Retained Resources

Once in a while, you will have an unfortunate situation of dealing with a major security incident or a data breach. It may require additional help just because of the size of the response you need to mount or because of some specific skill/expertise that you don't have in-house. For these, and other reasons, it is always a good idea to have a third party available for help, on a retainer basis.

So what should you look for in a third party while signing up for retainer services? Following are some considerations:

- Since attackers have no boundaries and incidents could be global in nature, make sure your incident response retainer provider has a global footprint, even if your business is regional or in one country.

- Also make sure they have people on staff who can speak major languages.

- Service Level Agreements (SLA) for providing services must be a key consideration. You want to make sure that help is available when you need it. Not a week after the incident.

- Also look for experience, history, and forensic capabilities of your vendor.

Beware of zero-cost retainer services because to provide SLA, the service provider has to maintain a bench that costs money.

7.3.3   Setting up Computer Security Incident Response Team (CSIRT)

Where should SOC analysts or CSIRT team take the lead and where should they collaborate during the incident response process? This section is a brief answer to this question and to establish a workflow.

Once SOC analysts declare an event as a security incident, the CSIRT takes the ownership of the incident, takes necessary actions and closes it. The objective of CSIRT is to execute a workflow for responding to the incidents once it is escalated by SOC analysts. The main reason for having a CSIRT is to keep SOC analysts primarily focused on threat monitoring activities instead of getting into response activities which may take a long time and may divert their attention away from their primary goal of threat monitoring and detection. A typical high level workflow for the CSIRT team is shown in Figure 7.1 that also shows collaboration between SOC analysts and the CSIRT.

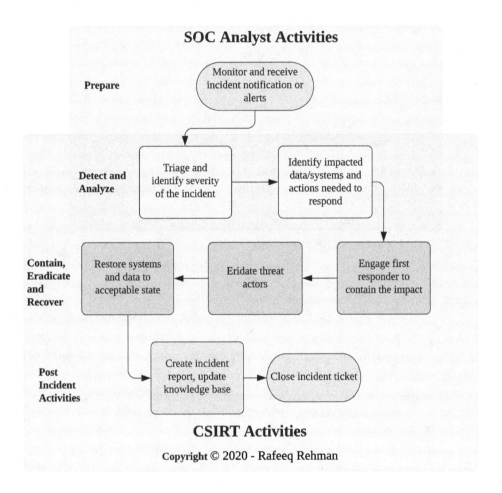

Figure 7.1: CSIRT Workflow

Note than the CSIRT team will be working with the SOC analysts in some phases of the incident response whereas it will take lead in containment, eradication, recovery and post incident activities. However, collaboration among all stakeholders is crucial during incident response and you should not strive for drawing hard lines for where the role of one team starts/ends as long as the responders are clear about who is the lead on certain activities.

ENISA and other organizations have published good material about CSIRT establishment, training, and handbooks in case you need further help [14].

7.3.4 Threat Hunting

While the majority of SOC work is reactive, starting with monitoring of activity and identifying threats in near-real time, proactive threat hunting plays a key role in SOC success. Threat hunting helps discover threats that are not evident from log or other telemetry data. Threat hunters look for anomalies or other clues as a starting point, assuming that a breach has already happened, and search for threat activity.

▋ The objective of threat hunting is to reduce dwell time and mean time to detection.

Threat hunting could be initiated in a number of different ways:

- Threat hunters could take data from anomaly detection systems like user and entity behavior analysis (UEBA) and search for reasons of anomaly.

- Using indicators of compromise from threat intelligence feeds.

- Advisories from government or industry organizations.

Dark Web Hunting

Threat hunting is done both inside of your network as well as outside on the dark web. Experienced threat hunters are usually able to determine if stolen data is being sold/traded on the dark web. If they find any stolen data, it gives them clues about when the data could have been stolen and what they need to look into to stop further bleeding.

Dark web hunting is also offered *as-a-service* by many vendors and could be a good option if you don't have internal threat hunters.

Threat Hunting with SOC Staff

Depending upon the size of SOC team, you could have dedicated threat hunters or you could also use tier-III analysts for threat hunting when they are able to spare time.

7.3.5 Preparing for a Data Breach

Preparing for data breach is the best thing anyone can do for themselves and for their organization. Preparations for data breaches include many activities. If these activities are not led by the SOC team, SOC needs to be part of these at minimum. Examples of activities for data breach preparation are as follows:

- Provide breach response training to staff, including incident handling for insider threats.

- Building and testing incident response processes.

- Conducting breach simulation exercises on a regular basis.

- Red team exercises to identify gaps in defensive controls.

- Building a first responder team and establishing a first responder training program.

- Budgeting for covering expenses of a data breach.

- Contracting with an incident response third party to help in case of a data breach.

- Purchasing a data breach insurance policy.

My suggestion is to create a quarterly schedule to test your preparedness for data breaches. You can use Table 7.2 as a starting point.

Quarter	List of activities
Q1	• Refresh training for data breach handling
Q2	• Data breach simulation exercises (internal) • Breach simulation for partners and supply chain (external)
Q3	• Red team exercise
Q4	• Review policies • Review insurance coverage and if it needs change in coverage

Table 7.2: Data breach preparedness testing

The data breach preparations should focus on the fact that sooner or later a data breach will happen and the organization should be ready to handle it.

7.3.6 Major Data Breach Stakeholders

Although major data breaches require a very coordinated response from all areas of the organization, typical major stakeholder are as follows.

- **Network** teams to monitor the network and make any changes during the response process.

- **Firewall Administrators** (and other security technology administrators)are part of incident response teams.

- **Desktop** management teams are also part of first responders, especially if endpoints are involved in data breach.

- **Server and Database** administrators

- **Legal** is typically involved in maintaining attorney-client privileges as well as evidence preservation for any litigation.

- **Human Resources** department may be involved during and after the data breach, especially when dealing with internal threat actors.

- **Public and investor relations** is always involved in effective external communications.

All major stakeholders should be part of preparations and exercises.

7.3.7 Major Activities as a Result of Data Breach Response

Following are some major activities that would occur as a response to data breach. It would be good to have people trained in these activities and making these part of your incident response plan.

- **Forensic and Investigation** - What happened, how it happened, who is behind it.

- **Evidence Collection and Preservation** - Major data breaches will follow law suites and evidence needs to be preserved so that it is acceptable in the court of law.

- **Law Enforcement Partnership** - Engage law enforcement agencies.

- **Compliance, Breach Notification and Public Relations** - When and who to send breach notification to, how to make public announcements.

- **Business Continuity and Disaster Recovery** - Ensure the business continues to operate. In some cases damaged systems may need to be recovered, for example, in the case of a ransomware attack.

- **Cyber Insurance** - Working with cyber insurance for claims.

So what you need to do? Think about the following:

- Create a liaison person for each team in a broader IT organization.

- Convey incident response process with other teams and make them part of table top exercises.

- Establish a "first responder" team and train them on basic tasks like how to create an image of a running system.

7.3.8 Forensic Capability

Some SOC organizations prefer to keep a base minimum level of forensic capability in-house and then contract an external vendor to provide additional forensic on as-needed basis. This strategy works well to manage costs as you may not need a full time forensic investigator on a daily basis (if you are managing a small to medium size SOC).

7.4 SOC Technology Infrastructure Management

An essential part of SOC day-to-day operations is managing the technology that SOC relies upon. These may be infrastructure like networks and servers, as well as applications and platforms. Just like other IT infrastructure, ITIL processes should be used for SOC infrastructure as well.

7.4.1 Change Management

SOC systems need changes and updates just like any other IT system. A change management process for SOC should address:

- Establish change management process following ITIL methodology. This process must be integrated into the overall IT change management process.

- Changes must be evaluated and approved before implementation. A backout option must be available for all changes.

- All patches to SIEM and other systems should be in the scope of change management.

- A special process for updating SIEM content, use cases and alerts should be established that ensure that all new alerts are well-tested and people are trained on what actions will be taken for new alerts.

- Always create a back-out strategy for changes.

If vulnerability management is part of the scope of your SOC, any changes to vulnerability scanning must also go through the change management process.

7.4.2   Problem Management

ITIL provides specific definition for *problem* and recommendations for *problem management*. A problem is basically a recurring issue that needs to be investigated to find the *root cause* and then fix it. In a SOC environment, recurring incidents of the same nature indicate an underlying problem in overall technology management. SOC staff should continuously evaluate incidents and find patterns that may point to a problem and then help solve it.

7.4.3   Business Continuity and Disaster Recovery (BC/DR) Exercises

Business Continuity and Disaster Recovery are essential for SOC planning and design as shown in section 6.7 on page 77. To validate and test BC/DR plans, you should:

1. Ensure BC/DR exercises are part of SOC policy.

2. Procedures are defined for conducting these exercises.

3. Exercises are conducted at least once a year. Twice a year would be better.

4. After each exercise, there must be a "lessons learned" meeting to identify required improvements.

The BC/DR exercises must demonstrate to meet recovery time objectives and recovery point objectives to be deemed as successful.

7.4.4   Patch Management

It would be better to leverage and follow corporate patch management processes for SOC. Most of the data breaches that leverage unpatched systems use vulnerabilities that are more than one year old [42]. While you don't want to be too aggressive, you don't want to be too slow either in applying patches to SOC systems.

7.4.5   Capacity Management

Telemetry data is even-increasing, new systems are added all the time, and businesses are expanding their digital footprint. All of this results in increased requirements for SOC. Capacity management is essential to ensure SOC is ready to take and process additional data and provide additional services. A good practice is to plan capacity enhancements at least one year ahead of time and use SOC governance structure to prioritize and make budget requests.

7.4.6   Penetration Testing

SOC infrastructure should be treated as crown jewels of an organization and should be tested rigorously for any vulnerabilities and weaknesses. Penetration testing is a minimum control for this purpose. You should also perform periodic architectural review of SOC infrastructure to ensure any weaknesses are identified and fixed in a timely manner.

7.5   Build and Improve Use Cases

Building and improving "use cases" is a continuous task for SOC to identify threats. Section 5.4 on page 57 provides a detailed guideline for building use cases.

New use cases are developed and existing ones are fine tuned/updated as a result of situations like:

- After addition of new log data sources.

- As a result of new threat intelligence pointing to certain threats that may be of interest to your organization.

- To expand threat detection capabilities of SOC as part of continuous improvement.

- Reduce excessive false-positive rate resulting from poorly designed use cases.

In any case, SOC should have a "content developer" role, either as a full time person or as part of tier-III responsibilities.

7.5.1 Identify Missing Log Data

One common issue with log management is detection of missing log data. Sometimes, a server would stop sending logs due to a change applied to the server. In other cases updates to firewall policies may be the culprit where a port used for sending log data is accidentally blocked. A mechanism should be put in place to detect these situations and identify missing log data.

One approach for detecting missing logs is to create a use case specific to that purpose that monitors all important log sources, especially the one that are either high-risk or needed for compliance reasons. The use case would generate alerts when a log source stops sending data for a specific time period. The time period could be decided based upon the tolerance for specific items.

Another approach is to use some machine learning (ML) methods to detect missing logs as an anomaly and generate alerts. The advantage with ML methods is that it can learn/tune itself if you use unsupervised learning techniques.

7.6 Stress and SOC Staff Burnout

SOC staff are dealing with threats and investigations on a regular basis every day. In many cases these threats are repetitive. Dealing with threats makes SOC staff stressed [26]. Stress and burnout are real problems and Thom Langford has written a blog about his personal experience as CISO coping with stress and its impact on his life which could be eye opening for many [28].

What is stress?

According to National Institute of Health, MedlinePlus [30], *"Stress is a feeling of emotional or physical tension. It can come from any event or thought that makes you feel frustrated, angry, or nervous. Stress is your body's reaction to a challenge or demand. In short bursts, stress can be positive, such as when it helps you avoid danger or meet a deadline. But when stress lasts for a long time, it may harm your health".*

Chronic stress results in burnout of SOC staff. Burnout is a state of mental and physical exhaustion due to prolonged stress that drains out energy.

- Burnout is a result of constant stress. If you find a co-worker calling sick often or coming late to work, it may be a sign of burnout.

- Burnout may also manifest in an otherwise efficient person taking longer to finish tasks.

SOC managers should not only take care of themselves against these very real issues but also make sure SOC staff is healthy with a good work-life balance. I can't emphasize enough how important this is for a successful SOC.

> **PITFALL: Is stress and burnout real?**
>
> As part of my research for this book, I had the opportunity to talk to medical doctors to better understand stress, how it works, and its impact on performance and productivity of people. After these discussions, I am even more convinced that this is an area that SOC managers and CISOs must know about and make it part of overall SOC planning. Ignoring implications of stress not only has dire consequences on individuals' life but also impacts success of a SOC.

7.6.1   How to Identify if SOC Staff is Stressed Out?

SOC managers need to understand stress and take actions to minimize its impact on SOC staff. Every person takes stress differently while living through the same type of experiences. Prolonged stress results in exhaustion and results in visible signs of damage to one's health. If you see a co-worker agitated, frustrated, or overwhelmed, it could be the first sign of stress.

7.6.2   What SOC Managers Can Do?

Well-being of SOC staff must be at the top of any SOC manager agenda. It is not only a good practice but is also essential for staff retention and operational efficiency of SOC. TO start with, managers must know:

- What causes stress and burnout?

- How to find if an employee is stressed out?

- What managers can do to address this issue?

One of the ways stress manifests in terms of physical health is hypertension. The research in this area is well documented and largely accepted [40].

Following are some actions that can reduce stress for SOC staff:

- Flexibility of working hours.

- Recognition of the work SOC staff does.

- Making sure staff take time for lunch and take breaks. They are not too much absorbed in work such that they forget to take breaks.

- Reduce console time for staff, rotate their duties.

- Provide some time where staff can work on "things they like" or on "problems they want to solve".

- Since triage of events could involve performing the same tasks over and over, work on tools and automation to minimize fatigue from these repetitive tasks. If you have not yet, consider investing in SOAR tools.

- Make sure staff members take vacation and other time off.

- Celebrate successes, no matter how small they are.

- It may not be a bad idea in investing in buying gym membership for SOC staff.

I would strongly recommend that each SOC should encourage SOC staff to check their blood pressure on regular basis, which could be a sign of stress, especially for young people. To address privacy concerns, an option should be provided to staff to buy and keep a blood pressure meter at home. Decent personal use equipment costs less than $100 and is a good investment in SOC staff health.

Another general recommendation is to increase awareness of stress among SOC staff. One way to do so is to purchase a few "stress posters" and place these on SOC walls as a constant reminder.

7.7   SOC Reporting and Metrics

Effective governance requires meaningful metrics and reporting. The project plan should include the following:

- Define a list of meaningful SOC metrics that show workload and effectiveness of SOC in achieving objectives (also means that SOC objectives should be defined in the first place!)
- How to automate data collection for metrics and avoid manual work
- Frequency for metrics and reporting
- Executive dashboards

The key to successful metrics and reporting is ensuring that these metrics and reports are meaningful and automated.

7.8   SOC and Compliance Needs

Almost all security compliance standards require log management, threat detection and incident response. Hence a SOC is always tied to compliance needs which the SOC managers need to fully understand to ensure successful audits. My suggestions are:

- Understand and list all compliance needs and relevant sections of standards/regulations where SOC has a role to play (e.g. PCI DSS).
- Get an agreement with internal compliance teams and/or auditors about what actions and reports they need to meet the compliance needs.
- Automate these reports and save historical copies.

The less time you spend on compliance, the better it is. A little upfront planning and automation will go a long way to achieve that goal.

7.9   SOC Integration Points

SOC does not live and operate in isolation and there are many integration points, not only from technology perspective but also for processes. Over the lifecycle of SOC, you will continuously be engaged in adding new integration as well as make the current integration more efficient. Following are some of the key areas that you should consider:

- New log sources
- Missing log detection
- Ticketing (could be internal as well as external)

- CSIRT teams

- Asset management

- Vulnerability scanning

- Crisis management

- Cloud providers

- External incident response retainer contracted firms

- Network Operations Center (NOC) as many incidents will require collaboration between NOC and SOC.

- Threat intelligence and information sharing, both internal and external to the organization.

- SOAR technologies (if these are part of your SOC environment).

7.10   Additional SOC Best Practices

This section is to list some of the best practices that are not discussed earlier in this chapter but would be very helpful in SOC operations.

7.10.1   Maintain SOC Runbook

A runbook is typically a collection of procedures and operations that SOC staff carries out. It is also used to keep track of SOC staff activities, build workflows, and as a reference. Effective runbooks enable new staff members to understand, troubleshoot and manage systems as well as handle exceptions/contingencies. You can have a runbook as printed copies or in electronic form.

7.10.2   Create and maintain a risk register

A risk register is used to maintain a list of known risks, associated mitigation controls, risk owners, probability, and impact. As a starting point, you can use a simple table like 7.3 or create a more sophisticated one.

Risk	Owner	Rating	Owner	Probability	Impact	Mitigation Controls

Table 7.3: A sample (simple) risk register

7.10.3   Knowledge Management, Wiki

An internal Wiki or a similar system is necessary for SOC staff to document any new items they learn, workarounds, known issues and other knowledge items that would be useful for SOC staff. When staff work in shifts, they are not always able to meet each other and exchange information. Wiki becomes very helpful in maintaining "tribal knowledge" and helps in resolving issues, especially for repeating incidents.

7.10.4   Staff Quality

Although you have a number of SOC analysts positions that you need to fill, but always prefer quality over quantity[50] even if you have to wait and even if it takes longer time to fill these jobs.

7.11   Chapter Summary and Recommendations

We have covered a lot of ground in this chapter as smooth and efficient operations is the most important part of any SOC. Following is the summary of crucial parts that contribute towards success of SOC.

- Importance of SOC governance can't be emphasized enough. This is the most critical success factor for long-term success.

- Hiring the right kind of people, training, managing their stress levels, and scheduling shifts is very critical as well.

- The most important process for SOC is incident detection and response. Building and improving use cases, automation and use of SOAR technologies is part of it.

- Applying ITIL processes to manage SOC infrastructure is quite important.

- Meaningful metrics, automated reports, and dashboards do help not only in meeting compliance needs but also facilitate effective communications across broader IT teams as well as business leadership.

- Last, but not the least, maintain a risk register, plan for next year, and always be ready to respond to data breaches.

8

SOC Staff Training and Skills Development

When Alexander joined the company as SOC manager, the first thing he realized was that most of the staff was not very enthusiastic about the work they did everyday. Although nobody was explicitly complaining, he would often hear *"can't wait for my shift to be over"* or *"thanks god it is Friday and I don't have to deal with this for next few days"*. While building his relationships across IT teams, he also heard that DevOps team have difficulty communicating with the SOC team about how they develop and deploy micro services in the Cloud.

Soon he realized that it is not that SOC staff is not capable or not qualified, it is just that they are tired of doing the same thing over and over without any opportunity to learn new things or do something different than routine tasks. He quickly put in place few programs including having a day for the staff to do whatever they wanted to do, a monthly hackathon [43] and a skills development program to enhance SOC staff knowledge in areas like Containers[12], Kubernetes [27][47] and edge computing. Soon he started seeing a much more cheerful team with a lot of new ideas of improvements to SOC and a much better communications with broad technology organization.

This is not an uncommon situation as we have seen in section 7.6 on page 93. Working as a SOC analyst is a stressful job. It also requires continuous skill updates and development as the technology changes. Focus of this chapter is to help you create an effective training and skills development program and identify major areas that should be included in the program.

> **Assumptions**
>
> At this point I am assuming that SOC analysts already have basic skills needed for regular SOC operations including log collection, SIEM, SOC processes etc.

8.1   How to Develop a Training and Skill Development Program?

While every SOC team is different in size and skill sets, my recommendation is that the skills development and training program should have some essential elements that are necessary for SOC analysts and other personnel working in the SOC. The recommended areas of skills are as follows:

- Foundational skills - These are the skills that are essential for every SOC professional to perform the job and understand the context of the situation.

- Networking - Fundamental knowledge about TCP/IP networking. Additional knowledge of protocols will be required if SOC is responsible for operational technologies and IoT.

- Risk management - Risk assessment fundamentals to enable SOC analysts make judgment calls on different types of alerts.

- Hands-on skills for basic tasks (e.g. packet capture, vulnerability scanning etc.). It is a good idea to make Kali Linux (or some other security focused Linux distribution) as a standard for hand-on skills development.

- Automating and scripting - a necessary trait to improve SOC efficiency over time.

- Threat landscape understanding, both strategic and tactical based upon data driven research from different reputable organizations.

- Certifications that may include CISSP, EC-Council Certified SOC Analyst and others on as needed basis.

- Fun stuff - doing projects that every person may be interested in, including hackathons on regular intervals to solve problems that otherwise are not considered.

8.2   Foundational Skills: A Refresher for Baseline Concepts

Following are some areas that every SOC professional should know about and get a better understanding. The information below is just a pointer and reader of this book should go and learn more about these areas.

8.2.1   Log Collection with Syslog

Syslog is the oldest and most commonly used manner of gathering log data from different operating systems. Many applications also use Syslog to send event logs. Internet Engineering Task Force (IETF)[1]. published RFC standard documents for Syslog protocol that all SOC professionals should read and understand [19].

8.2.2   Cyber Kill Chain

Lockheed Martin created a framework known as *the Cyber Kill Chain* which is a registered trademark for the company. The model specifies seven stages or steps that an adversary would follow to achieve their objectives, usually data exfiltration. The Cyber Kill Chain is a useful tool to understand the severity of an attack and the urgency of actions needed to stop an attacker. These seven stages of the Cyber Kill Chain are as follows.

---

[1]For more information refer to ietf.org

1. Reconnaissance

2. Weaponization

3. Delivery

4. Exploitation

5. Installation

6. Command and Control

7. Action on objectives

A lot has been written about the Cyber Kill Chain [29] in different texts and online sources. There is a possibility that the software or SIEM may already have implemented some of these concepts in categorization of attacks at different levels.

When creating a curriculum for SOC staff training, an introduction to the Cyber Kill Chain and how to utilize its principles in the SOC operations will be a good idea.

8.2.3 PKI Basics

Public Key Cryptography (PKI) is an essential area that every SOC analyst should be proficient in. PKI is used in almost every aspect of Cybersecurity threat monitoring. Include at least the following in the curriculum.

- Symmetric and Asymmetric Algorithms

- Key Exchange

- SSL and TLS Protocols

- Digital certificates

- Public and private certificates

- Certificate Authority (CA)

- Different between encryption and hashing

- Digital signatures

- Common encryption algorithms

- Common attacks on PKI and known vulnerabilities

As an advanced subject to cryptography, some SOC analysts may also be interested in understanding Quantum Computing and Quantum Key Distribution.

8.2.4 Understanding RESTful API

Most of the Cloud Service Providers provide log data through API (Application Programming Interface) instead of traditional Syslog messages. REST (REpresentational State Transfer) is based upon HTTP protocol to enable machine to machine communications. It is very likely that your SOC is gathering some log data using RESTful API or will do so. From the training perspective, it is useful to include:

- How RESTful APIs work?

- How to test API using either web browser or command line tools like curl?

- Some level of understanding of OAuth and OpenID protocols.

- Security APIs and common attacks against APIs

8.2.5 Understanding Containers

It is very likely that some applications in your organization are built on what is called *containers* [12] infrastructure. If you have an internal DevOps team, it is highly likely that containers are being used in your organization in one way or the other. Understanding containers is very crucial for modern SOC teams as containers are dynamically created and destroyed based upon demand/load on an application. Unlike regular servers that have fixed IP addresses and stay more or less static, a container may appear, send log messages and then disappear. This is important for SOC analysts for proper identification of sources of log data and then taking appropriate actions.

In the training curriculum, include at least the following:

- What are containers and how they work.

- Container registries and docker.

- Starting, stopping and interacting with containers.

8.3 TCP/IP Network

Yes it is obvious that security professionals do understand the TCP/IP protocol. However you will be surprised in many cases that their knowledge may not have that much depth as needed to fully understand network anomalies, packet headers, RFCs and so on. Following are recommendations for a minimal training and knowledge development on TCP/IP protocols.

8.3.1 IP Packet Headers

IP packet header (layer 3 and above) as well as Ethernet frame structure is essential. Consider the following to be included in the course material.

- Understanding a data packet structure (hearder and payload).

- Ethernet frame structure.

- IP header structure and meaning of different header fields.

- Transport layer header structure (TCP, UDP).

- Application layer headers for common applications (at least DNS, DHCP, HTTP, SMTP).

- ICMP and how it works.

- Introduction of Internet standard documents (RFC) and IETF. Relevant RFCs for IP, TCP, UDP, ICMP, HTTP, DNS, SMTP etc.

- VPNs and how different types of VPNs work.

- IPv6 and IPv4 differences. Basic understanding of IPv6.

- Use of packet sniffers like tcpdump, Wireshark[2].

---

[2]wireshark.org

8.3.2 Network Diagnostic Utilities

Common network diagnostic utilities that should be included in training are:

- Ping
- Trace, traceroute
- nslookup, dig
- route, traceroute
- curl

8.3.3 Common Application Level Protocols

A good understanding of common application layer protocols and respective data packet headers is quite useful.

- DNS
- DHCP
- HTTP
- SMTP
- SSH
- Voice protocols

8.4 Understanding Risk Management

Risk assessment is a fundamental job for SOC. Use the following for training curriculum:

- Understanding differences of basic terminology (risk, vulnerability, threat, loss, etc.).
- Qualitative and quantitative risk
- Risk management frameworks (NIST, FAIR, COSO, ISO)

8.5 MITRE ATT&CK Framework

MITRE ATT&CK framework[3] is a knowledge base of tactics and techniques. It is based upon real life observations and provides a basis for building controls as well as threat modeling when creating use cases. Like the Cyber Kill Chain, the ATT&CK framework is also very useful in building a deeper understanding of adversaries. The current version of the framework include twelve (12) techniques and many sub-techniques. The main techniques are listed below:

1. Initial Access
2. Execution
3. Persistence
4. Privilege Escalation
5. Defense Evasion

---

[3]https://attack.mitre.org/

6. Credential Access

7. Discovery

8. Lateral Movement

9. Collection

10. Command and Control

11. Exfiltration

12. Impact

A good understanding of MITRE ATT&CK framework will significantly enhance SOC capability not only to effectively respond to attacks but also help other teams better prepare and proactively stop different types of attacks.

8.6   Helpful Tool

Following is a list of commonly used hands-on tools.

- **Port Scanning and Asset Discovery** with nmap.

- **Transfer data** with curl using various network protocols.

- **Domain name search** using command line and online tools including nslookup, dig, different types of DNS records, whois tools.

- Effective use of ping and trace

- **Scanning suspicious files and URLs** using virustotal[4].

8.7   Kali Linux

Kali Linux is a security-focused Linux distribution with a large number of security tools bundled. Many teams use tools available on Kali Linux for incident response processes as well as for general testing and training. Including a training about how to taking machine image or perform basic pen testing is very useful for tier-2 and tier-3 SOC analysts.

8.8   Automation and Shell Scripting Basics

Improving SOC efficiency should be one of the objectives of every SOC team. For this, at least some people in SOC team should be proficient in:

- Automating with cron, bolt and other tools.

- Windows PowerShell

- Windows Remote Management

- Python

---

[4]https://www.virustotal.com/gui/

8.9 Process for Building Use Cases

This is already discussed in earlier parts of this book. For references please see sections 1.10 and 3.4.2 about threat modeling, and section 5.4 on use case development. Fundamentally, there are two ways to make decision about which use cases to develop and implement:

- Take a look at available log sources and decide what information you can get from this data.

- Perform a threat modeling, decide what is crucial for you to monitor.

If you are using threat modeling, the MITRE ATT&CK framework will also be very helpful.

With the machine learning (ML) options, you should also train SOC tier-III analysts on ML algorithms so that they can build use cases based upon behavior and anomalies instead of signatures. They would need to build models and train these models (in case of supervised learning) or let these models train themselves (using unsupervised learning).

8.10 Research Reports

Many organizations publish reports on a regular basis. Keeping an eye on these reports will be useful to understand the changing threat landscape. Following are some categories of these reports:

- Insider Threat

- Attack Patterns and Trends - Verizon Data Breach Investigations Report (DBIR)

- PCI Compliance Reports

- Cost of Data Breaches - Ponemon and other reports

- Threat Actor Specific Reports - Many security vendors publish reports that are specific different threat actors. If you believe you are a target of nation-state actors, these reports would be useful for your SOC staff.

8.11 Industry Certifications

In some cases you may also want to make certification option available to your SOC staff. There are many common certifications that you can decide on, starting with certified ethical hacker, CISSP and others. I would suggest decide upon a certification path based upon the focus of your SOC. Certifications for Cloud technologies are excellent as more and more applications/data is moving to the Cloud.

8.12 Chapter Summary and Recommendations

- Cybersecurity field is changing very rapidly. Updating SOC staff skills must be a key part of effective SOC management.

- For each tier of SOC staff, managers should define an essential set of curriculum/skill and provide training opportunities to the staff.

- Providing training may be part of the job role for Tier-III analysts.

- In addition to conceptual training, the SOC staff must also have hands-on skills for common tools to effectively respond to incidents.

- Use list of areas in this chapter as a baseline to build training and learning programs. The program should continuously evolve as responsibilities of SOC evolve.

- For specialized SOC (e.g. a SOC for connected vehicles or SOC for IoT or Operational Technologies), domain knowledge is also necessary in addition to common SOC practices.

Part III

Continuous Improvement

9

Threat Intelligence and Threat Hunting

Threat intelligence, also referred to Cyber Threat Intelligence (CTI), is defined in a number of ways. In simple words, threat intelligence helps you understand adversaries and protect your organization in a better way. Threat intelligence helps you understand who are the actors, their methods of attack and indicators showing attack occurred in the past or is in progress. The objective of threat intelligence is to make your security program more effective against these attacks.

As you can imagine, the threat actors keep on changing their tactics, techniques, and procedures (TTPs). Unless you get a timely and continuous stream of information and effective ways to utilize it, protecting your organizations against these attacks is a daunting task. The field of threat intelligence has evolved significantly in the past few years. Many Threat Intelligence Platforms (TIP) are available as commercial products as well as in the free space. These platforms provide capabilities for integration into security devices and platforms like IPS, SIEM, Firewalls and others. If you have not recently looked into the available TIP options, I would strongly advise to do research into available options and start a pilot program, maybe initially with free threat intelligence feeds. Effective use of threat intelligence is absolutely crucial not only for the overall security program but also for SOC.

This chapter will enable you to understand what threat intelligence is, what options are available to use threat intelligence, threat intelligence platforms and how/where to get started.

9.1 Sources of Threat Intelligence

Typically you will receive threat intelligence from three main source types as listed below:

- Internal - Security devices, SOC analysts, operations teams, internal honeypots and deception technologies etc.

- External - External sources include open source and commercial threat intelligence feeds. External threat intelligence also comes from dark web hunting.

- Partner - Typical partners are industry associations like ISACs[1] which are non-profit organizations to gather, analyze and share information in different industry sectors. For example, FS-ISAC is an organization for the financial industry. Typically you have to apply for an ISAC membership.

The key to these data types is that they should be relevant to a particular organization and the threat landscape they are facing.

9.2 Types of Threat Intelligence

There are three basic types of threat intelligence as listed below. You should be looking for all three types for effective SOC operations. Figure 9.1 shows these types whereas a brief description is also provided below.

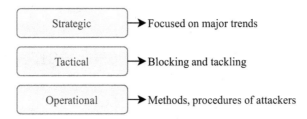

Figure 9.1: Summary of different types of threat intelligence

- Strategic intelligence is related to understanding trends. For example, Verizon DBIR shows that most of the threats are motivated by financial gains. However, in certain industries espionage may be a significant motivation as well. Understanding these strategic factors help you focus your attention in certain areas. Many organizations/vendors publish threat intelligence research reports that should be part of SOC staff continuous training to keep them aware of major trends.

- Tactical intelligence shows indicators of compromise and helps you make tactical decisions like blocking an IP address, looking for certain hash codes, blocking a certain malware communication and so on. Many open source and commercial threat intelligence feeds provide tactical intelligence in real time.

- Operational Intelligence is about tactics, techniques and procedures (TTPs) of the attackers and is crucial to understand their capabilities and methods of attacks. Most attacks are multi-stage where the attack may start with a phishing email, followed by installing a first-stage malware, then downloading second stage malware, collecting data and finally exfiltrating data. Attackers may also use multiple attack vectors at different stages. Understanding these operational capabilities will help you break the attack and stop attackers before data is exfiltrated.

Do you need all of the threat intelligence types listed above? Yes, as these serve different purposes. Even when you don't have a budget for a commercial threat intelligence platform or threat feeds, you should at least have a strategy of obtaining and utilizing open source threat intelligence and work with your industry ISACs.

Threat Intelligence and NIST Cybersecurity Framework Tiers

If you are using NIST Cybersecurity Framework (CSF), the way you collect, use and share threat intelligence is an essential factor in determining NIST CSF implementation tier [33].

---

[1]Information Sharing and Analysis Centers

> **Where to get threat intelligence from?**
>
> Threat intelligence should be collected from three "zones": Global, industry-specific and local. Intelligence from vendors may be considered as Global. ISACs provide industry-specific threat intelligence. Local intelligence is what you create from your own vulnerabilities, weaknesses, and attacks you are seeing.

9.3 Intelligence Sharing and Traffic Light Protocol (TLP)

The *Traffic Light Protocol* is a *labelling* mechanism used by the producers of threat intelligence information to instruct the recipient about how the information should be further shared [1][46]. It uses four labels as listed below:

1. **TLP:RED** - This label is used for information that should not be further shared with anyone outside the group decided by the producer of the information.

2. **TLP:AMBER** - This information can be shared within the organization, clients and customers on a need-to-know basis.

3. **TLP:GREEN** - This information can be shared within a community but should not be published to the public, for example, on the Internet.

4. **TLP:WHITE** - This is the information that can be published to the public and usually poses no risk of misuse.

The producers usually place the TLP labels at the top of the documents before sharing with appropriate consumers. It is assumed that the consumers will respect the labeling and will restrict or share the information accordingly.

SOC analysts receive labeled threat intelligence from different sources like US-CERT, CISA and other organizations. Understanding the TLP protocol is necessary for further sharing of the information with internal or external entities.

9.4 Strategic Threat Intelligence Sources

Think of strategic threat intelligence as understanding of the threat landscape, major trends in your specific industry sector, threat actors and their motives in a bigger picture. For example, strategic threat intelligence should tell you if you need to worry about opportunistic attackers or more targeted attacks from state-backed actors. Or what is your risk related to insider threat actors? Is the latest trend includes attacks on web applications, point of sales (POS) systems, or ransomware?

So how you get the strategic threat intelligence and keep your SOC analysts updated on it. Although there are commercial sources, but you can achieve goals with many open source strategic threat intelligence sources. Threat intelligence reports from reliable sources/vendors is one of these options. Some sources are listed below:

- Verizon data breach investigations report (DBIR)[2] is the main source of trends and strategic intelligence data.

---

[2]Check https://enterprise.verizon.com/resources/reports/dbir/ of google search on DBIR

- Cyentia Institute publishes research reports[3] as well as maintains a library[4] of reports published by other organizations.

- Ponemon Institute Library[5] is another good source of research information.

Note that strategic intelligence is the one that will help you create/update your strategy rather than day-to-day blocking and tackling of threats and incidents, which is usually done through tactical and operational threat intelligence.

9.5   Tactical and Operational Threat Intelligence Sources

Tactical and operational threat intelligence includes threat intelligence feeds (many times delivered through threat intelligence platforms), indicators of compromise, TTPs (tactics, techniques, and procedures) as shared by different CERT (computer emergency response team) organizations as well as through ISACs memberships.

9.6   Commercial and Open Source Threat Intelligence Feeds

Many vendors include threat intelligence feeds with their security commercial products. If you buy threat intelligence platform, you will get some feeds with it. However, many smaller SOC teams rely on open source feeds due to budget constraints. However, open source intelligence feeds may not be as reliable and diligently curated as commercial feeds.

9.7   STIX and TAXII

Structured Threat Information eXpression or STIX and Trusted Automated eXchange of Intelligence Information or TAXII are designed for packaging and sharing threat intelligence information. STIX is a standardized way of packaging information in a machine readable format. TAXII on the other hand defines how the information should be transmitted/received.

Adopting standards makes it easier for all entities to share and use information. These standards have been adopted worldwide and most of the threat intelligence platforms use STIX and TAXII for their threat intelligence feeds. STIX is developed by MITRE and OASIS Cyber Threat Intelligence (CTI) Committee. The latest version of STIX is 2.1 and it uses a JSON based schema/profile for threat intelligence. When look at a STIX package, it will contain information like:

- Campaigns

- Names and descriptions

- Threat indicators

- Dates when the package was created and modified

- Malware information, ports, protocols, IP addresses

The above is just a sample. For detailed information and samples please refer to CTI documentation on Github (https://oasis-open.github.io/cti-documentation/).

---

[3]https://www.cyentia.com/research/
[4]https://library.cyentia.com/
[5]https://www.ponemon.org/research/ponemon-library/

TAXII is based upon the concept of *producer* and *consumer*. The producer creates threat intelligence in STIX format and the consumer takes and utilizes it. Consider TAXII as a client-server mechanism. On the producer side, you will use a TAXII client to publish information to a TAXII server. On the consumer side, you will use a TAXII client to get information from a TAXII server. The consumer side can work as a *subscriber* to threat intelligence feeds as well as *poll* information from TAXII servers using a *request-response* mechanism.

Knowledge of STIX and TAXII is essential for SOC staff and it should be part of the training curriculum.

Typically a TAXII server, whether hosted online or internally, will have a URL that the TAXII client will point to. Many TAXII clients have the capability to "discover" threat intelligence feeds that a TAXII server provides and you should be able to pick and choose the feeds. You should also be able to choose a polling interval for the feeds that you are interested in. You may also need to purchase feeds if these are commercial before you can subscribe.

9.8 Threat Intelligence Platforms

Threat intelligence platforms (TIP) enable organizations to collect, aggregate, analyze and use threat intelligence data from multiple sources and use this data to strengthen defenses in real time. A TIP is an essential component of any modern SOC. Threat intelligence platforms are typically used to collect all threat feeds in one place using STIX/TAXII as well as other methods. SOC also uses TIP to share intelligence data with trusted circles of other organizations as well as ISACs. Some organizations also use TIP to integrate threat data with other security technologies like firewalls to take actions in real time without any human intervention. However this functionality is not widely used.

If you want to get a feel about how threat intelligence platforms work, you may want to try one or more of the following:

- Anamoli/STAXX - As of writing this book, STAXX[6] is available as a free download from Anomali. STAXX will give you a good idea about how to subscribe to threat intelligence feeds, confidence levels, etc.

- The MISP Platform - The MISP Threat Sharing platform[7] is an open source threat intelligence sharing platform built on open standards [37].

- MineMeld - You may also think about trying MineMeld[32] to check some capabilities of threat intelligence platforms.

Like other technologies, any TIP is as good as people using it. This basically means that the technology itself will not solve anything until you have SOC staff who can use this technology effectively.

9.9 Threat Hunting

Reactive techniques of log analysis for threat detection are not sufficient for an effective SOC. Why? Log based detection technologies are not always perfect. More and more experts now agree that it is prudent to assume that a breach has already happened and that the existing security technologies and controls are not able to detect it. Proactive threat hunting is a set of activities used to uncover the presence of attackers inside your network that were otherwise

---

[6]https://www.anomali.com/resources/staxx
[7]https://www.misp-project.org/

not detected using existing security controls and methods. While doing so, threat hunters focus on discovering tactics, techniques, and procedures used by the attackers [22]. While a typical SIEM and log based methods are used to detect threats in a reactive manner, the assumption for threat hunting is that a breach has already happened and threat actors are already inside the network.

Threat hunters typically create hypotheses and then try to prove these in a methodical manner. They may also rely on internal or external threat intelligence to create their hypotheses. Threat hunting activities could be performed inside your own network, Cloud environment as well as outside of your network. An example of outside activities is dark web hunting.

When you plan SOC, creating a dedicated or semi-dedicated role for proactive threat hunting is a good idea. You should also define threat hunting policies, procedures as well as guidelines.

9.10   Theat Hunting: Where to Get Started?

Threat hunters use many ways as their starting point to initiate threat hunting. Figure 9.2 shows some of these starting points for proactive threat hunting.

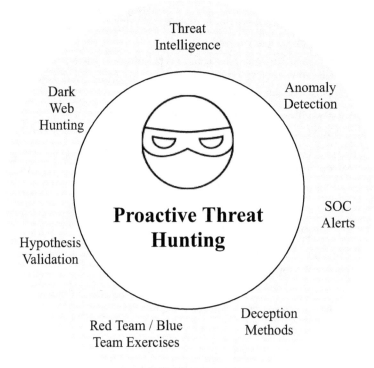

Figure 9.2: Threat Hunting

9.10.1   Threat Intelligence

Many times you get information about new threats through open source or commercial threat intelligence sources and you are wondering: Are we victims of this threat actor? Or should we investigate whether an indicator of compromise (IOC) exists within my network. So many times threat hunting starts with threat intelligence sources.

9.10.2 Anomaly Detection

Many times you find something that "looks" abnormal or out of place and that may trigger a thought to investigate it. Modern technologies are also capable of detecting anomalies that include:

- Netflow analysis tools are able to detect anomalies in network traffic, including large amounts of data transfers.

- Many SIEM technologies are now capable of detecting anomalies in user and entity behavior.

- Connecting to different geographic regions may also show an anomaly worth investigating.

- Many times anomaly detection is key to insider threat detection because internal actors have legitimate access to computer systems.

Threat hunters would usually use interesting anomalies as a starting point for taking next actions.

9.10.3 SOC Alerts

Tier III SOC analysts may have threat hunting included in their job description and may use SOC alerts as a starting point for threat hunting. They are usually very familiar with trends because of their involvement in SOC and incident detection/response.

9.10.4 Deception Methods

Deception technologies are an evolution of honeypots, are much more effective and easier to implement. These technologies are capable of early breach detection. However, alerts from these technologies can also be the basis for threat hunting.

9.10.5 Red Team/ Black Team Exercises

Finding weaknesses in defenses as a result of red team and blue team exercises is a useful method to develop hypotheses for threat hunting.

9.10.6 Dark Web Hunting

Proactive threat hunting is not confined within network boundaries or within Cloud environments. Effective threat hunting requires that you assume data is stolen and is being traded on the dark web.

Although dark web hunting capability can be built in-house, it may not be a cost effective proposition. Dark web hunting is offered as a service by commercial vendors.

9.11 Chapter Summary and Recommendations

- Threat intelligence in an essential part of any modern SOC.

- For effective management of threats, you need strategic, tactical, and operational intelligence.

- Traffic Light Protocol uses a color coding method to enable the source of threat intelligence label documents and provide guidelines to recipients about how far and wide threat intelligence can be shared downstream.

- STIX and TAXII are mechanisms to enable machines to exchange threat intelligence feeds. STIX 2.0 is based upon JSON and TAXII is a protocol to exchange STIX packages.

- Threat Intelligence Platforms are used to collect, aggregate, analyze, search and share threat intelligence both at human and machine level.

- Proactive threat hunting is an essential function of a modern SOC.

10

Measuring Efficiency and Metrics

Effective metrics are used for measurement of progress. In the case of SOC, metrics demonstrate the value of SOC investments. Survey reports show that many organizations don't use metrics or use metrics that are ineffective and fail to show SOC value in overall risk reduction.

While every organization is different and can choose a list of relevant metrics, following are main categories that you can consider while planning SOC operations.

- Activity based metrics

- Outcome based metrics

- Governance and Compliance metrics

- Health and availability metrics

A prudent strategy for selecting relevant metrics is consider:

- Select simplest metrics first before considering more complex ones.

- Make sure the SOC governance organization approves selection of metrics or updating the list.

- Automate SOC metrics so that it does not become a manual nightmare.

- Ensure that metrics are used to understand the state of SOC operations and achieving some arbitrary metric value does not become an objective in itself.

In the following sections, you can find a list of metrics in each of these categories. This will help you pick and choose the ones that are relevant in your case.

10.1 Activity Metrics

Activity based metrics are not as useful as outcome based metrics but still convey useful information that could be helpful in improving efficiency of SOC operations. Some of these metrics are as listed below:

- Size of Log Data

- Total Number of Log Sources

- Number of Incidents

- Number of Escalations to Tier-II/III

- Incidents Caused by Known Vulnerabilities

- Custom Rules

In the early stage of building SOC, you may start with activity-based metrics but eventually you should focus on outcome based metrics.

10.2   Outcome Based Metrics

The outcome based metrics are the most useful ones. These show data that is actually indicative of appropriate risk management.

- Time to Detection - This is one of the metrics that all SOC managers should strive to measure and decrease time for detection. It requires diligence, red/blue/purple team exercises.

- Time to Contain-Recover - Improving this metric requires strong coordination with broader IT teams and first responders.

- Incident Detection in Kill-Chain Phases - Number of incidents detected in different phases of the kill chain. This metric may be a little hard but it tells an excellent story about the effectiveness of SOC if it is able to detect the majority of incidents in the early phases of Kill Chain.

- Mean Time To Restore (MTTR) - This metric is a good measure for incident response.

- Reduction of False Positives - Either percentage or absolute number will be a good measure.

- Threat Hunting - Finding the unknown is becoming more and more important and shows effectiveness of threat hunting strategy and capabilities.

- Behavior based detection of incidents vs. correlation based incident detection

- Usefulness of Threat Intelligence Feeds - Showing how threat intelligence is helping in detection, response, and in threat hunting. This is to establish the value of threat intelligence.

- Contribution to IT Operations - How SOC is helping different information technology teams in detection of non-security events and incidents, e.g. detection of misconfigurations in network, software, or business applications.

Outcome based metrics are the most valuable. SOC manages should ensure that these are automated because manual work could lead to errors and usefulness of these metrics.

10.3   Governance and Compliance Metrics

SOC always has some component of complying with different industry standards and/or government laws. In addition SOC governance activities will benefit from measuring SOC efficiency. Some additional metrics for governance and compliance activities are listed below.

- Cost per Incident

- Staff Retention

- Staff Training

- SOC Budget

- Threat Intelligence Sharing - Sharing intelligence is important internally as well as externally.

- Integration with Other Systems including Vulnerability Management, Cloud security and others.

- Log Retention

10.4   SOC Health and Availability Metrics

Following metrics are related to basic up-keeping of security operations center health and proper functioning.

- Uptime

- Patching and Upgrades

- Missing Log Data

These metrics should be aligned with similar metrics used in the organization.

10.5   Automating Metrics and Reporting

As discussed above, any metrics or reports that need manual work are ultimately going to create more work for SOC staff and will contain errors. When deciding metrics for your organization, please make sure you have a means for automating data collection and presentation to the end user.

10.6   Hiring Full Time Employees (FTE) vs. Automation

In general, my suggestion for SOC managers is to always prefer automation over hiring more people. When workload increases and you are tempted to hire more analysts, think about what can be automated or activities that are not creating value that could be dropped.

10.7   Chapter Summary and Recommendations

- In the initial phases of SOC, start with easy and activity-based metrics.

- Gradually move towards outcome based metrics. Start with a small set and then gradually increase over time.

- Although it may not seem useful initially, creating metrics that show SOC value outside of "security" can be very helpful building credibility and relationships with other IT teams.

- Always automate data collection instead of manual work.

—Open source is not just about software, it is a social movement that has brought more people out of poverty than any other initiative in the history of humankind. It is the biggest equalizer that has enabled ordinary people to get access to sophisticated technologies and build their careers which otherwise could never have happened.

Rafeeq Rehman

11

Open Source Solutions for SOC

While money plays a deciding role in whether you buy a commercial tool or go with open source, many times the decision of using commercial or open source tools is also about control. Open source tools are more suited for *builders* who are looking for more controls about modifying software tools to meet certain needs.

11.1 What is Open Source Software?

Open source software provides you source code that you can compile and modify to meet your needs. However, if you make any changes, you may have some restrictions on what changes you can make and if you need to share your modifications with the other open source communities. While using open source software, please read the software license carefully to avoid any risk to your organization. Please note that open source software still has copyrights. This text is not a guideline or advice on legal matters with the open source software so you should get proper legal advice, especially when you modify open source software or cross-link it with your proprietary software.

11.1.1 Is Open Source Software Free?

An open source software is not always "free" and may need license cost. In other cases, you may want to purchase "support" for open source software. Many open source software vendors make money from support costs instead of selling the actual software.

11.2 Selection Criteria for Open Source Software

While you have some assurance that a commercial software is supported by the vendors, it may not always be the case for the open source software. Following are some considerations for selecting open source software tools.

1. **Open source license model** - Open source software comes with different types of licensing models. Some are very friendly whereas others could be quite restrictive.

2. **Who is behind the open source project** - An established non-profit organization managing the open source software is a good sign. Many people start a project as open source and then turn it into a commercial version after getting a following, leaving early adopters in a fix. For example, projects supported by Apache Software Foundation (apache.org) or Free Software Foundation (fsf.org) would be a good bet.

3. **Maturity and industry adoption** - A software which is widely adopted in the industry and has a history of maturity/continuity is better than the ones with low adoption rate. It will be easier to find staff knowledgeable in mature and widely adopted software in case you lose existing staff members.

4. **Development activity** - A good indication for open source projects is to see how actively new features are added and how often updates are made.

5. **Bug fixes and security updates** - No software is 100% bug free. New vulnerabilities are always identified. You want to make sure that the open source software development teams promptly release fixes.

11.3   Open Source SIEM Tools

A number of tools are available in the Open source that may be considered for very small and low-budget security teams. However, as mentioned earlier, there is a large cost in terms of time consumed in managing these software and dealing with integration issues.

11.3.1   Apache Metron

If you are looking for a scalable and comprehensive open source SIEM platform with capabilities to ingest large numbers of data sources and integrate threat intelligence, Apache Metron (https://metron.apache.org/) is a great choice. Metron is built with Hadoop and provides options for full packet capture and behavior analysis among other options.

11.3.2   OSSEC

OSSEC (https://www.ossec.net/) is an open source and free software available for multiple platforms. Many organizations use it as Host Intrusion Detection System. It is a mature platform and can be easily integrated with other SIEM systems.

11.3.3   ELK Stack

ELK (https://www.elastic.co/what-is/elk-stack) is an acronym for Elasticsearch, Logstash, and Kibana. When combined, these tools provide a comprehensive environment for collecting, analyzing and storing log data. You can also purchase support for ELK stack. Downloads are available from https://www.elastic.co/downloads.

11.4   Vulnerability Management

OpenSCAP is a set of tools for compliance and vulnerability management. You can also use this tool set for vulnerability scanning of containers. It is available at https://www.open-scap.org/.

Another popular vulnerability management tool is OpenVAS (https://www.openvas.org/) that enables vulnerability scanning and management. It relies on a number of other open source tools integrated into a comprehensive platform.

11.5   Intrusion Detection

To feed data into SOC/SIEM, following are some of the open source technologies that are well tested and have significant following.

11.5.1   Snort

Snort (https://snort.org/) is a rule based engine and has been very popular among security professionals for almost two decades.

11.5.2   BRO IDS, Zeek

Bro IDS, now known as Zeek, is another open source network security monitoring tool[1]. It includes many user contributed packages as well.

11.5.3   OSSEC

OSSEC is already described earlier in this chapter. It is a powerful host based intrusion detection (HIDS) system.

11.5.4   Suricata

Suricata (https://suricata-ids.org/) is another open source IDS/IPS which is easy to integrate into SIEM technologies with JSON formatted alert data.

11.6   Knowledge Management and Wiki

Managing knowledge base is always a necessity for SOC operations. SOC analysts learn new techniques and methods of dealing with certain situations. A knowledge management system helps maintain this information and make it available for analysts in other shifts.

Wiki is a great solution for managing knowledge. Wiki software enables users to create and edit knowledge articles, search, and make enhancements to existing information.

Although there are many open source Wiki and other open source knowledge management software available, I would recommend Media Wiki (https://www.mediawiki.org/) which is also the foundation of Wikipedia, provides styles, and can be integrated into LDAP sources for authentication.

11.7   EDR and OSQuery

Endpoint Detection and Response (EDR) tools are helpful in incident response. OSQuery (https://github.com/osquery/osquery) (https://osquery.io/) is an open source tool to provide visibility into end points with a SQL like syntax. There are many examples of using OSQuery

---

[1]https://zeek.org/

across the enterprise[2]. You can check running processes, browser plugins and other useful information of data with OSQuery to detect presence of attackers that otherwise may be invisible to different security tools.

11.8   Open Source Packet Capture

Molch (https://molo.ch/) is one of the solutions that can capture, index, search packet data as well as provide an interface for graphs and sessions.

11.9   Digital Forensic and Incident Response Tools, Linux Distributions

- KALI Linux Kali Linux (https://www.kali.org/) is a popular Linux distribution used by security professionals. It combines a variety of tools into a single distribution that you can install on laptops and use it for responding to incidents, forensic analysis, taking machines images and other routine tasks.

- **Deft toolkit Linux distribution** - Forensic analysis, incident management tool kit - http://www.deftlinux.net/

- **SANS Investigative Forensics Toolkit (SIFT)** - SIFT[3] is available as pre-configures workstation package, is free and open source.

- **CAINE** - CAINE[4] is another digital forensic Linux distribution with many tools combined into a single distribution.

11.10   Chapter Summary and Recommendations

- Open source is not new. World runs on Linux, which is an open source operating system. Many tools are available for the Security Operations Center as well.

- When using open source, it is wise to establish a criteria for selecting open source technologies that should take into account the license, maturity of the product, development activity, and industry following among others.

- If you are building SOC on budget and have experienced staff, going open source may not be a bad idea.

- When selecting open source stack, you can start with an open source SIEM solution. Apache Metron is a scalable solution that can provide excellent functionality and scale of Hadoop.

- Data collection with open source solutions is an option with multiple IDS/IPS solutions, end point information gathering, full packet capture.

- Many Linux distributions bundle digital forensic tools that can be handy for SOC staff, even when you are relying mostly on commercial products.

---

[2]https://medium.com/palantir/osquery-across-the-enterprise-3c3c9d13ec55
[3]https://digital-forensics.sans.org/community/downloads
[4]https://www.caine-live.net/

Bibliography

[1] FIRST Traffic Light Protocol Special Interest Group (TLP-SIG). *Traffic Light Protocol (TLP)*. 2018. URL: https://www.first.org/tlp/.

[2] American Public Power Association. *Cyber Incident Response Playbook*. 2019. URL: https://www.publicpower.org/system/files/documents/Public-Power-Cyber-Incident-Response-Playbook.pdf.

[3] AXELOS. *ITIL - Information Technology Infrastructure Library*. 2018. URL: https://en.wikipedia.org/wiki/ITIL.

[4] Ayehu. *Top 5 Cyber Security Incident Response Playbooks*. 2020. URL: https://ayehu.com/cyber-security-incident-response-automation/top-5-cyber-security-incident-response-playbooks/.

[5] Girish Bhat. *Introducing Splunk Security Use-Cases*. 2016. URL: https://www.splunk.com/en_us/blog/security/introducing-splunk-security-use-cases.html.

[6] *BrightTalk web portal*. 2020. URL: https://brighttalk.com.

[7] Creative Commons. *Creative Common Licenses*. URL: https://creativecommons.org/licenses/.

[8] IR Consortium. *Incident Response Consortium Playbooks*. 2020. URL: https://www.incidentresponse.com/playbooks/.

[9] *Coursera online training programs*. 2018. URL: https://coursera.org.

[10] Chris Crowley. "Common and Best Practices forSecurity Operations Centers:Results of the 2019 SOCSurvey". SANS Institute, 2019.

[11] J. Burbank D. Mills J. Martin and W. Kasch. *Network Time Protocol Version 4: Protocol and Algorithms Specification*. 2010. URL: https://tools.ietf.org/html/rfc5905.

[12] Docker. *What is a Container?* 2020. URL: https://www.docker.com/resources/what-container.

[13] *EDX online training programs*. 2018. URL: https://edx.org.

[14] ENISA. *Setting up a CSIRT*. 2020. URL: https://www.enisa.europa.eu/topics/trainings-for-cybersecurity-specialists/online-training-material/setting-up-a-csirt.

[15] ENISA. *Trainings for Cyber Security Specialists*. 2018. URL: https://www.enisa.europa.eu/topics/trainings-for-cybersecurity-specialists/online-training-material.

[16] EUGDPR. *The EU General Data Protection Regulation (GDPR)*. 2018. URL: https://eugdpr.org/.

[17] Daniel Frye. "Effective Use Case Modeling for Security Information and Event Management". SANS, 2019.

[18] Gartner. *Security Orchestration, Automation and Response (SOAR)*. 2020. URL: https://www.gartner.com/en/information-technology/glossary/security-orchestration-automation-response-soar.

[19] R. Gerhards. *The Syslog Protocol - RFP 5424*. 2009.
URL: `https://tools.ietf.org/html/rfc5424`.

[20] Paul Cichonski Tom Millar Tim Grance and Karen Scarfone.
Computer SecurityIncident Handling Guide. 2014. URL: `https://nvlpubs.nist.gov/nistpubs/SpecialPublications/NIST.SP.800-61r2.pdf`.

[21] Y. Rekhter B. Moskowitz D. Karrenberg G. J. de Groot and E. Lear.
Address Allocation for Private Internets. 1996.
URL: `https://tools.ietf.org/html/rfc1918`.

[22] Dan Gunter. *Applied Threat Hunting: Why Should You Hunt*. 2020.
URL: `https://www.linkedin.com/pulse/applied-threat-hunting-why-should-you-hunt-dan-gunter`.

[23] Infosec Institute. *Top 6 SIEM Use Cases*. 2018.
URL: `https://resources.infosecinstitute.com/top-6-seim-use-cases/`.

[24] SANS Institute. *GIAC Computer Forensics Certifications*. 2020.
URL: `https://digital-forensics.sans.org/certification`.

[25] ISACA. *COBIT 2019*. 2018. URL: `www.isaca.org/cobit/`.

[26] Dan Kaplan. *The art of recognizing and surviving SOC burnout*. technical report.
Siemplify, 2020.

[27] Kubernetes.io. *Contaiiner Orchestration*. 2020. URL: `https://kubernetes.io/`.

[28] Thom Langford. *Drowning, Not Waving. . .* 2019.
URL: `https://thomlangford.com/2019/02/18/drowning-not-waving/`.

[29] Lockheed Martin. *The Cyber Kill Chain*. 2020. URL: `https://www.lockheedmartin.com/en-us/capabilities/cyber/cyber-kill-chain.html`.

[30] MedlinePlus. *Stress and your health*. 2019.
URL: `https://medlineplus.gov/ency/article/003211.htm`.

[31] Trend Micro.
Cyberattacks from the Frontlines: Incident Response Playbook for Beginners. 2020.
URL: `https://www.trendmicro.com/vinfo/us/security/news/managed-detection-and-response/cyberattacks-from-the-frontlines-incident-response-playbook-for-beginners`.

[32] Palo Alto Networks. *MineMeld Threat Intelligence Sharing*. 2018.
URL: `https://www.paloaltonetworks.com/products/secure-the-network/subscriptions/minemeld`.

[33] NIST. *NIST Cyber Security Framework*. 2018.
URL: `https://www.nist.gov/cyberframework/framework`.

[34] NIST. *NIST Internet time service*. URL: `https://www.nist.gov/pml/time-and-frequency-division/services/internet-time-service-its`.

[35] NTP. *NTP: The Network Time Protocol*. 2014. URL: `http://www.ntp.org/`.

[36] OASIS. *The MQTT Protocol Specifications*. 2018. URL: `http://mqtt.org/`.

[37] MISP Project. *MISP - Open Source Threat Intelligence Platform and Open Standards For Threat Information Sharing*. 2018. URL: `https://www.misp-project.org`.

[38] Rsyslog. *Rsyslog, A fast system for log processing and forwarding*. 2018.
URL: `https://www.rsyslog.com/`.

[39] Simon Sinek. *Start with Why: How Great Leaders Inspire Everyone to Take Action*.
2009.

[40] Tania Spruil. *Chronic Psychosocial Stress and Hypertension*. Springer, 2010.

[41] *Udacity online training programs*. 2018. URL: `https://udacity.come`.

[42] Verizon. *Verizon Data Breach Investigations Report - DBIR*.
URL: `https://enterprise.verizon.com/resources/reports/dbir/`.

[43] Wikipedia. *Hackathon*. 2020. URL: `https://en.wikipedia.org/wiki/Hackathon`.

[44] Wikipedia. *Heating, ventilation, and air conditioning*. URL: https://en.wikipedia.org/wiki/Heating,_ventilation,_and_air_conditioning.

[45] Wikipedia. *SMART criteria*. URL: https://en.wikipedia.org/wiki/SMART_criteria.

[46] Wikipedia. *Traffic Light Protocol*. 2018. URL: https://en.wikipedia.org/wiki/Traffic_Light_Protocol.

[47] Wikipedia. *What is Kubernetes*. 2020. URL: https://en.wikipedia.org/wiki/Kubernetes.

[48] Sydni Williams-Shaw. *How to build an incident response playbook*. 2019. URL: https://swimlane.com/blog/incident-response-playbook.

[49] Carson Zimmerman. *Practical SOC Metrics*. 2019. URL: https://www.first.org/resources/papers/conf2019/Public__SOC-Metrics-for-FIRST-v07-002-.pdf.

[50] Carson Zimmerman. *Ten strategies for a world class Cybersecurity Operations Center*. 2014. URL: https://www.mitre.org/sites/default/files/publications/pr-13-1028-mitre-10-strategies-cyber-ops-center.pdf.

Index

www.ingramcontent.com/pod-product-compliance
Lightning Source LLC
LaVergne TN
LVHW081528050326
832903LV00025B/1689